Clerical Assistant Exam

Prepare for Success!

Angelo Tropea

Copyright 2019 by Angelo Tropea
Sections of this book have appeared in prior publications by the same author.
All rights reserved. No part of this book may be reproduced in any form or by any electronic or mechanical means, including information storage and retrieval systems without permission in writing from the publisher, except by a reviewer, who may quote brief passages in a review.

ISBN: 9781071106426

CLERICAL ASSISTANT

Please note

Exams developed by the Office of Court Administration are carefully and professionally crafted and further refined to separate unprepared candidates and candidates with limited ability from candidates who have superior ability and who have prepared well.

The exams are <u>not</u> "general knowledge" or simple aptitude exams. Serious preparation and a well thought out plan for tackling the different types of questions within the prescribed timeframe are both advisable and necessary for success.

Your decision to study with this book already has set you apart from candidates who will rush into the test unprepared.

Now that you have this book, take advantage of its benefits. Make this book your friend.

Study with it every day from now until the date of the test.

According to the 2019 exam announcement (Exam Numbers: 45-813 and 55-813):

"This **computer-based, multiple-choice examination** will be administered throughout New York State at PSI Test Centers...."

Although the format of the questions will be different from the previous written exams, the subject matter will almost be the same. A good understanding of the content of the different areas and understanding of how to answer the questions will greatly increase your chances of scoring high.

Although one might think that the number of extremely long or complex filing and record-keeping questions might be reduced by a computer-based exam, we cannot assume this will be the case. The secret to success is to study well and be ready for any type of question (and in any format) they might ask.

CONTENTS

1. Clerical Assistant Job and Exam Pay Grades / 4

2. Filing Questions / 9

3. Clerical Checking / 31

4. Court Record Keeping / 49

5. Reading, Understanding and Interpreting Written Material / 73

6. Number Facility / 80

7. Preparing Written Material / 89

8. Applying Facts and Information to Given Situations / 92

9. Coding and Decoding / 97

10. Practice Test Questions / 104

11. Practice Test Answers / 128

12. Practice Test Answer Key / 152

CLERICAL ASSISTANT

CLERICAL ASSISTANT JOB AND EXAM **1**

PAY GRADES FOR CLERICAL ASSISTANT SERIES OF TITLES (April 2019 estimated pay)

Title	Pay Grade	Beginning Pay	Max Pay with Longevity Pay
Court Office Assistant (Discontinued earmarked entry-level title)	10	35,545	53,500
Senior Court Office Assistant (Discontinued earmarked promotional title)	12	39,898	59,410
Clerical Assistant (NEW 2019 entry-level title which replaces the old Court Office Assistant, Keyboarding, and Data Recording Assistant titles)	12	39,898	59,410

All persons in the above titles who are in a permanent position are eligible to sit for the Court Clerk (pay grade 18) and Senior Court Clerk (pay grade 21) exams. Court Clerks can promote by means of exams to Associate Court Clerk (pay grade 23) and Principal Court Clerk (pay grade 26).

COURT CLERK SERIES OF TITLES
(April 2019 estimated pay)**

Title	Pay Grade	Beginning Pay*	Max Pay with Longevity Pay**
Court Clerk	18	56,045	81,686
Senior Court Clerk	21	65,652	94,857
Associate Court Clerk	23	73,020	104,790
Principal Court Clerk	26	85,806	121,662

** Additional pay (Geographic Differential) up to approximately $4,000 is also paid in designated counties.

CLERICAL ASSISTANT

Clerical Assistant Job and Benefits

The exams for the old Court Office Assistant series of exams were similar, with some differences. We expect that the Clerical Assistant exams will be like the old series of exams (EXCEPT that the new exams will be computer-based). The Clerical Assistant exam is open to the general public and often leads (by way of promotional exams) to the Court Assistant, Senior Clerical Assistant I and II, and even higher Clerk titles (Senior Court Clerk, Associate Court Clerk, and Principal Court Clerk).

All the above titles may be located in courts of every county of New York State (in Court Clerks' Offices, Commissioners of Jurors' Offices, law libraries, administrative offices and other places in the NYS Unified Court System).

Yearly pay increases are according to union contracts. Geographic pay differential is also often added to the regular salary. Annual leave (vacation days) are 20 days per year to start. Vacation days increase one day per year for the first seven years (totaling 27 days after seven years.) Sick days with pay are also provided.

NYS court employees may choose from a variety of health insurance plans. Each employee contributes a portion of the insurance premiums by means of a payroll deduction. Prescriptions are also included. Many unions provide vision and dental benefits.

Court employees are eligible for Social Security benefits and a pension from New York State. Employees contribute a portion of their salary toward the state pension. Employees may also contribute to a deferred compensation plan. Contributions are not taxed the year they are contributed.

Union membership benefits and dental insurance for Clerical Assistants assigned to New York City courts is provided by DC 37 Local 1070. In other parts of the state, other unions, such as CSEA, represent these titles.

Many Clerical Assistants (formerly Court Office Assistants) promote to higher Court Clerk positions. It is not uncommon to find employees originally in these titles earning three or four times their starting salaries.

Applications for all exams must be submitted according to the official exam announcement. (**There is a strict filing deadline**.)

For complete and current information, please visit:
www.nycourts.gov/careers/

CLERICAL ASSISTANT

Please check also for any update to the following nycourts.gov advice that appears in the Clerical Assistant exam announcements:

"CANDIDATES SHOULD CONTACT THE OFFICE OF COURT ADMINISTRATION AT (212) 428-2580 OR EXAMUNIT@NYCOURTS.GOV NO LATER THAN JULY 9, 2019 IF THEY HAVE NOT RECEIVED THEIR SELF-SCHEDULING LINK."

IMPORTANT

Read the official exam announcement carefully and follow directions, including applying within the application period and with the correct exam number.

For complete and current information, please visit:
www.nycourts.gov/careers/

CLERICAL ASSISTANT

TYPES OF QUESTIONS ON EXAMS*

What should I study?

Please read carefully the following descriptions of the types of questions that were listed on the exam announcement.*

Filing

These questions assess candidates' ability to arrange information into files according to categories specified by the directions in alphabetical, numerical and chronological order. Questions are based on the completed files.

Clerical Checking

These questions assess candidates' ability to distinguish between sets of names, numbers, letters and/or codes which are almost exactly like. There are three sets of information which may appear in different fonts. Candidates are asked to compare the information in the three sets and identify whether the sets differ. Candidates must use the directions provided to determine the correct answer.

Court Record Keeping

These questions assess candidates' ability to read, combine, and manipulate written information organized from several sources. Candidates will be presented with different types of tables, which contain names, numbers, codes and other information, and must combine and organize the information to answer specific questions.

Reading, Understanding and Interpreting Written Material

These questions assess candidates' ability to understand brief written passages. Candidates will be provided with short written passages from which words or phrases have been removed. Candidates will be required to select from four alternatives the word or phrase that logically completes the sentence within the passage when inserted for the missing word or phrase.

Number Facility

These questions assess candidates' ability to perform basic calculations involving addition, subtraction, multiplication, division and percentages. These questions do not require use of a calculator and calculators will not be permitted at the test center.

CLERICAL ASSISTANT

Preparing Written Material
These questions assess candidates' ability to apply rules of English grammar, usage, punctuation and sentence structure. Candidates will be presented with a series of sentences and must select the sentence that is most correct in accordance with standard English grammar, usage, punctuation and sentence structure.

Applying Facts and Information to Given Situations
These questions assess candidates' ability to use the information provided and apply it to a specific situation defined by a given set of facts. Each question contains a brief paragraph which describes a regulation, policy or procedure similar to what a Clerical Assistant may encounter on the job. All of the information needed to answer the questions is contained in the paragraph and in the description of the situation.

Coding and Decoding
These questions assess applicants' ability to use written sets of directions to encode information and use coded information for keeping records. Applicants will be presented with a table of coded information and then be asked to apply a set of coding rules to encode information accurately.

---

* Question descriptions are from prior OCA exam announcements (NYS Court Office Assistant Exam Announcement (2014), NYS Senior Court Office Assistant Exam Announcement (2014), NYS Court Assistant Exam Announcement (2010), NYS Supervising Court Office Assistant Exam Announcement (2010), Clerical Assistant Exam Announcement 2019.

CLERICAL ASSISTANT

FILING QUESTIONS 2

These questions assess candidates' ability to arrange information into files according to categories specified by the directions in alphabetical, numerical and chronological order. Questions are based on the completed files.*

CLERICAL ASSISTANT

FILING QUESTIONS

Filing questions test a candidate's ability to arrange information into files according to categories specified by the directions. Questions are based on the completed files. **Knowledge of alphabetical, numerical and chronological order is required.**

FILING QUESTION 1 (A Simple Example)

Directions:

Below is a list of 10 employees, the date each was hired, and the employee ID number.

First, prepare 3 lists of the employees in
1. alphabetical order by last name
2. ID order (numerical order)
3. date hired order (oldest date to most recent date)

After preparing the above lists, answer the 5 questions that follow. (You will **not** be graded on the lists that you prepare. You will **only** be graded on how you answer the 5 questions).

NAME OF EMPLOYEE	ID NUMBER	DATE HIRED
Benson, Harry	788543	6/7/1989
Williams, Richard	387562	3/9/1992
Houston, Robert	675499	7/8/1973
Jones, Anne	776123	9/4/1987
Baynes, Charles	438292	3/2/1982
King, David	276409	8/9/1989
Houston, Susan	387922	8/9/1989
Yard, Mary	729487	6/2/1999
Sussman, Barbara	380329	7/8/2004
Levine, Frances	346186	9/3/2003

Questions:

1. The name of the sixth employee on the NAME OF EMPLOYEE alphabetical list is:
A. Jones, Anne
B. King, David
C. Levine, Frances
D. Sussman, Barbara

2. The name of the fourth person on the DATE HIRED chronological list is:
A. Jones, Anne
B. Benson, Harry
C. Houston, Robert
D. Houston, Susan

3. The name of the employee who is number 3 on the ID NUMBER numerical order list is:
A. Sussman, Barbara
B. Levine, Frances
C. Williams, Richard
D. Houston, Susan

CLERICAL ASSISTANT

4. The name of the employee who is number 4 on the NAME OF EMPLOYEE alphabetical list is:
A. Houston, Robert
B. Houston, Susan
C. Jones, Anne
D. King, David

5. The date of hire of the seventh employee on the ID NUMBER numerical order list is:
A. 3/2/1982
B. 6/2/1999
C. 7/8/1973
D. 7/8/2004

(Answers are on page 14.)

Directly following this paragraph is the **WRONG** way to organize the employee name category. **TOO MUCH WRITING!** – Only the **Employee name** is needed to alphabetize the names.

If other information is needed to answer the questions, we can go back to the original information provided and obtain the required information. On the test you will have longer lists and **not enough time** to write out everything.

LIST OF EMPLOYEES (WRONG WAY! IT CONTAINS TOO MUCH INFORMATION)

Employee Name	ID Number	Date Hired
Baynes	438292	3/2/1982
Benson	788543	6/7/1989
Houston, Robert	675499	7/8/1973
Houston, Susan	387922	8/9/1989
Jones	776123	9/4/1987
King	276409	8/9/1989
Levine	346186	9/3/2003

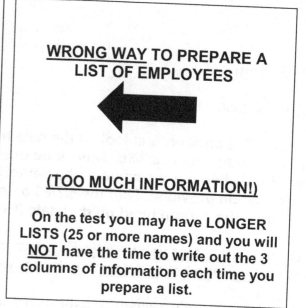

WRONG WAY TO PREPARE A LIST OF EMPLOYEES

(TOO MUCH INFORMATION!)

On the test you may have LONGER LISTS (25 or more names) and you will **NOT** have the time to write out the 3 columns of information each time you prepare a list.

The **three** files in the requested and **correct format** are as shown on the next page.

Note that we did **NOT** write out the corresponding 2 columns of information for the **employee name list** (shaded example on next page). We only wrote out the employee name. Also, we did not write out the corresponding 2 columns for the ID Number list and the Date Hired list.

CLERICAL ASSISTANT

Correct Employee Name List

Employee Name
Baynes
Benson
Houston, Robert
Houston, Susan
Jones
King
Levine

Correct ID Number List

ID Number
276409
346186
380329
387562
387922
438292
675499

Correct Date Hired List

Date Hired
7/8/1973
3/2/1982
9/4/1987
6/7/1989
8/9/1989 Howard
8/9/1989 King
3/9/1992

Answers for Simple Filing Question 1:

1. B (King)

2. B (Benson, Harry)

To get this answer, first look at the date hired list that you prepared. The fourth "date hired" on the list is 6/7/89. This alone does not tell you the name of the person hired on 6/7/89. To find out the name of the person hired on 6/7/89, look at the original information provided. Find the 6/7/89 date and then look across the row to find out the name of the person hired on that date (Benson, Harry).

<u>On the actual test you may find a number of questions where you will need to refer to more than one list to determine the answer.</u>

(To also correctly answer questions 3 and 5, looking at more than one list is also necessary.)

3. A (Sussman, Barbara)

4. B (Houston, Susan)

5. C (7/8/1973)

CLERICAL ASSISTANT

FILING QUESTION 2

Below is a list of employees, the date each was hired, their employee ID number and the department to which they are assigned.

First, prepare 4 lists of the employees in
  1. alphabetical order by last name list
  2. ID order (numerical order) list
  3. date hired order list
  4. department order (and also alphabetical order of employees in that department) list

After preparing the above lists, answer the 19 questions that follow. (You will **not** be graded on the lists that you prepare. You will only be graded on how you answer the 19 questions).

NAME	DATE HIRED	EMPLOYEE NUMBER	DEPARTMENT
Williams, Joyce	6/17/2004	56892	Judgments
Jones, John	7/3/1988	98234	Calendar
Grady, Jim	5/4/1977	24889	Small Claims
Portnoy, Thomas	9/8/1999	10273	Appeals
Abrams, Jack	4/5/1984	35999	Special Term
Young, Wanda	3/9/2001	64908	Landlord and Tenant
Oliver, Henry	5/6/1989	27890	Special Term
Darden, Kim	5/1/1983	28777	Calendar
Holmes, Eleanor	6/6/2002	89012	Warrants
Qualms, Nancy	4/5/1976	92098	Special Term
Ryker, Irma	4/7/2003	24567	Judgments
Zoolander, David	3/2/2003	61435	Warrants
Vawn, George	6/4/1973	78657	Calendar
Davidson, Bob	8/5/1996	45912	Landlord and Tenant
Moon, Kim	4/4/1982	77777	General Clerk
Feinstein, Josette	5/3/2001	39329	Special Term
Brady, Sam	2/5/2000	91432	Landlord and Tenant
Jameson, Erik	2/2/1987	87953	Judgments
Underhill, Frank	1/7/2001	22598	Appeals
Peters, Tim	3/2/1995	73999	Warrants
Wong, Peter	7/9/1985	34876	General Clerk
Chin, Robert	3/2/1996	44354	Small Claims
Kevaney, Pamela	7/4/1978	86345	Judgments
Ericson, Vivian	9/4/1998	99876	Special Term
Battle, James	3/1/1985	00241	Appeals

CLERICAL ASSISTANT

Suggested Procedure

1. Draw the boxes for the 26 letters of the alphabet (including "y" and "z"). See below.
2. Label the boxes "a - z".
3. Write each last name in the appropriate box (according to the first letter of the last name).
4. Count the number of names in the boxes and the number of names on the original list. <u>They must be the same number (to make sure that you haven't skipped any names).</u>
5. Write in a column format the alphabetical list.
6. **Quickly count the number of names in the column and make sure it is the same number as the number of names on the original list.**
7. Answer the questions.

(Remember: You will **not** be graded on how you prepare the lists. You will only be graded on how you answer the questions.)

ALPHABETICAL ORDER (Write the last name only. This will save time and space.)

a	b	c	d	e	f
g	h	i	j	k	l
m	n	o	p	q	r
s	t	u	v	w	x

y   z

See the following page for an example of how the boxes should be filled out and for an example of the completed list.

CLERICAL ASSISTANT

(Last Name Alphabetical list - prepared by You!)

a	b	c	d	e	f
Abrahms	Battle Brady	Chin	Darden Davidson	Ericson	Feinstein
g	h	i	j	k	l
Grady	Holmes		Jamison Jones	Kevaney	
m	n	o	p	q	r
Moon		Oliver	Peters Portnoy	Qualmes	Ryker
s	t	u	v	w	x
		Underhill	Vawn	Williams Wong	

y Young   z Zoolander

Abrams
Battle
Brady
Chin
Darden
Davidson
Ericson
Feinstein
Grady
Holmes
Jamison
Jones
Kevaney
Moon
Oliver
Peters
Portnoy
Qualms
Ryker
Underhill
Vawn
Williams
Wong
Young
Zoolander

The list on the left is the way the correctly completed list should look like.

You need this list to answer the questions.

Sometimes to answer a question you will need this list AND the original list provided by the exam question.

Although there will be a few questions that you can answer without preparing a special list, there will be many more for which you will need the list to answer them both quickly and correctly. The time to prepare the list will pay off in both speed and accuracy (AND A HIGHER SCORE - <u>AND FASTER HIRING</u>.)

CLERICAL ASSISTANT

HELPFUL TECHNIQUES TO REMEMBER

1. FILING BY ALPHABETICAL ORDER

Unless instructed otherwise:

1. Alphabetize employee names by their LAST name

    James, John (JAMES is the last name)

    John James (There is no comma, therefore James is the last name)

2. Re-write as little information as possible (Just write the LAST names unless there are two or more people with the same last name.)

3. Do NOT re-write unnecessary columns (information about an employee can be obtained from the information provided in the original columns.)

4. After you finish putting a column in order, COUNT the number of names and agree it to the number of names provided by the question to make certain you have not skipped any names.

2. FILING BY DATE HIRED

Unless instructed otherwise:

1. The OLDEST DATE is listed first (The MOST RECENT DATE is listed last.)

2. When you write a date, try to use the date format "6-5-06" instead of "6/5/06" to avoid confusing the "/" with the number "1".

3. Do NOT re-write unnecessary columns (information about a hire date can be obtained from the information provided in the original columns.)

4. After you finish putting a column in order, COUNT the number of dates and agree it to the number of dates provided by the question to make certain you have not skipped any dates.

CLERICAL ASSISTANT

3. FILING BY TITLE (and then EMPLOYEE NAME ORDER WITHIN THAT TITLE)

Unless instructed otherwise:

1. List the titles in alphabetical order and **ALSO** list the employees within that title in last name alphabetical order.

2. Re-write as little information as possible (Just write the LAST names unless there are two or more people with the same last name.)

3. Do NOT re-write unnecessary columns (information about an employee in a title can be obtained from the information provided in the original columns.)

4. After you finish putting a column in order, COUNT the number of names and titles and agree them to the number of names provided by the question to make certain you haven't skipped any names or titles.

4. FILING BY ASSIGNMENT

(and then EMPLOYEE NAME ORDER WITHIN THAT ASSIGNMENT)

Use the same techniques as in number "3" above.

At the test site try to make the best use of whatever scrap paper (if any) is provided for your use during the test.

Note: the test is "computer-based". It is not known if they will provide any scrap paper.

CLERICAL ASSISTANT

FILING QUESTION 2

1. The third name in the Last Name Alphabetical File is:
   A. Battle, James
   B. Brady, Sam
   C. Chin, Robert
   D. Grady, Jim

2. The twenty-second name in the Last Name Alphabetical File is:
   A. Vawn, George
   B. Underhill, Frank
   C. Williams, Joyce
   D. Wong, Peter

3. The name that comes directly after Feinstein, Josette in the Last Name Alphabetical File is:
   A. Holmes, Eleanor
   B. Feinstein, Kim
   C. Jones, John
   D. None of the above.

4. The name that is number 14 in the Last Name Alphabetical File is:
   A. Kevaney, Pamela
   B. Oliver, Henry
   C. Davidson, Bob
   D. Moon, Kim

5. Which of the following four statements is not correct?
   A. Chin, Robert is the fourth name in the Last Name Alphabetical File.
   B. Darden, Kim comes before Ericson, Vivian in the Last Name Alphabetical File.
   C. Feinstein, Josette comes directly after Davidson, Bob in the Last Name Alphabetical File.
   D. Battle, James is the second name in the Last Name Alphabetical File.

6. The tenth employee on the alphabetical list was hired on:
   A. 4/5/1976
   B. 5/1/1983
   C. 7/3/1988
   D. 6/6/2002

7. The seventh employee on the alphabetical list works in the _____ department.
   A. General Clerk
   B. Special Term
   C. Landlord and Tenant
   D. Calendar

8. The employee with employee number 77777 is the _____ employee on the alphabetical list.
   A. thirteenth
   B. fourteenth
   C. fifteenth
   D. sixteenth

9. Which of the following four statements is correct?
   A. Zoolander, David is not the name of the last employee on the alphabetical list.
   B. On the alphabetical list employee James, John is listed after Jamison, Erik.
   C. On the alphabetical list employee Davidson, Bob is listed after employee Darden, Kim.
   D. There are 24 names of employees on the alphabetical list.

10. George Vawn was hired on _____.
    A. 4/6/1973
    B. 6/4/1978
    C. 6/4/1973
    D. None of the above.

CLERICAL ASSISTANT

(Date hired list prepared by You!)

(In this example I decided to organize the boxes in decades to make the sorting out of the dates and their subsequent listing in date order easier.)

1970s	1980s	1990s	2000s
6/4/73	4/4/82		
4/5/76	5/1/83	2/2/95	6/5/2000
		3/2/96	1/7/2001
5/4/77	4/5/84		
	3/1/85		3/9/2001
7/4/78	7/9/85	8/5/96	
			5/3/2001
	2/2/87	9/4/98	6/6/2002
		9/8/99	3/2/2003
	7/3/88		
	5/6/89		4/7/2003
			6/17/2004

11. The employee whose hired date is listed number 6 on the chronological date hired list has employee number ____.
A. 64908   C. 35999
B. 77777   D. 28777

12. The employee hired date of 3/2/1996 is listed number ____ on the chronological list of dates hired.
A. 12   C. 15
B. 13   D. 14

13. The employee Darden, Kim is listed number ____ on the chronological list of dates hired.
A. 4   C. 6
B. 5   D. 7

6/4/73
4/5/76
5/4/77
7/4/78
4/4/82
5/1/83
4/5/84
3/1/85
7/9/85
2/2/87
7/3/88
5/6/89
3/2/95
3/2/96
8/5/96
9/4/98
9/8/99
2/5/2000
1/7/2001
3/9/2001
5/3/2001
6/6/2002
3/2/2003
4/7/2003
6/17/2004

CLERICAL ASSISTANT

(Employee Number Order list prepared by You!)

(In this example I decided to organize the boxes by 10,000s: for example, 0-10,000, 10,001-20,000, 20,001-30,000, 30,001-40,000, etc.)

0-10,000	10-20	20-30	30-40	40-50
00241	10273	22598 24567 24899 27890 28777	34876 35999 39329	44354 45912
50-60	60-70	70-80	80-90	90-100
56892	61435 64908	73999 77777 78657	86345 87953 89012	91432 92098 98234 99876

14. The name of the employee whose employee number is listed number 18 on the employee number order list is ____.
A. Kevaney, Pamela   C. Jameson, Erik
B. Brady, Sam   D. Vawn, George

15. Employee Chin Robert's employee number is listed number ___ on the chronological list of employee numbers.
A. 10   C. 11
B. 13   D. 12

16. The employee whose employee number is number 10 on the chronological list of employee numbers works in the ___ department.
A. General Clerk   C. Calendar
B. Special Term   D. Small Claims

00241
10273
22598
24567
24899
27890
28777
34876
35999
39329
44354
45912
56892
61435
64908
73999
77777
78657
86345
87953
89012
91432
92098
98234
99876

CLERICAL ASSISTANT

(List of Employees by Department prepared by You!)

(In this example I decided to make each box a department, which I listed in alphabetical order. When I listed the employees in their box (department), I was careful to also place them in correct alphabetical order)

Appeals	Calendar	General Clerk	Judgments
Battle Portnoy Underhill	Darden Jones Vawn	Moon Wong	Jameson Kevaney Ryker Williams
Landlord and Tenant Brady Davidson Young	Small Claims Chin Grady	Special Term Abrams Ericson Feinstein Oliver Qualms	Warrants Holmes Peters Zoolander

17. The employee name that appears as number 12 on the employee list (by department order) is _____.
A. Zoolander, David
B. Brady, Sam
C. Ryker, Irma
D. Williams, Joyce

18. The department which has the greatest number of employees assigned to it is _____.
A. Landlord and Tenant
B. Special Term
C. Judgments
D. Small Claims

19. The employee who is listed second in the Landlord and Tenant Department in the employee list (by department order) is _____.
A. Brady
B. Davidson
C. Young
D. Chin

Appeals- Battle
Portnoy
Underhill
Calendar- Darden
Jones
Vawn
General Clerk- Moon
Wong
Judgments- Jameson
Kevaney
Ryker
Williams
Landlord and Tenant-
Brady
Davidson
Young
Small Claims- Chin
Grady
Special Term- Abrams
Ericson
Feinstein
Oliver
Qualms
Warrants- Holmes
Peters
Zoolander

CLERICAL ASSISTANT

Answers for Filing Question 2: (Correct answers are underlined and in bold.)

1. The third name in the Last Name Alphabetical File is:
A. Battle, James   **B. Brady, Sam**   C. Chin, Robert   D. Grady, Jim

2. The twenty-second name in the Last Name Alphabetical File is:
A. Vawn, George
B. Underhill, Frank
C. Williams, Joyce
D. Wong, Peter

3. The name that comes directly after Feinstein, Josette in the Last Name Alphabetical File is:
A. Holmes, Eleanor
B. Feinstein, Kim
C. Jones, John
D. None of the above *(Brady)*

4. The name that is number 14 in the Last Name Alphabetical File is:
A. Kevany, Pamela   B. Oliver, Henry   C. Davidson, Bob   **D. Moon, Kim**

5. Which of the following four statements is not correct?
A. Chin, Robert is the fourth name in the Last Name Alphabetical File.
B. Darden, Kim comes before Ericson, Vivian in the Last Name Alphabetical File.
C. Feinstein, Josette comes directly after Davidson, Bob in the Last Name Alphabetical File.
D. Battle, James is the second name in the Last Name Alphabetical File.

6. The tenth employee on the alphabetical list was hired on:
A. 4/5/1976   B. 5/1/1983   C. 7/3/1988   **D. 6/6/2002**

7. The seventh employee on the alphabetical list works in the _____ department.
A. General Clerk   **B. Special Term**   C. Landlord and Tenant   D. Calendar

8. The employee with employee number 77777 is the _____ employee on the alphabetical list.
A. thirteenth   **B. fourteenth**   C. fifteenth   D. sixteenth

9. Which of the following four statements is correct?
A. Zoolander, David is not the name of the last employee on the alphabetical list.
B. On the alphabetical list employee James, John is listed after Jamison, Erik.
C. On alphabetical list employee Davidson, Bob is listed after employee Darden, Kim.
D. There are 24 names of employees on the alphabetical list.

10. George Vawn was hired on _____.
A. 4/6/1973
B. 6/4/1978
C. 6/4/1973
D. None of the above.

CLERICAL ASSISTANT

11. The employee whose hired date is listed number 6 on the chronological date hired list has employee number____.
    A. 64908
    B. 77777
    C. 35999
    D. 28777

12. The employee hired date of 3/2/1996 is listed number ____ on the chronological list of dates hired.
    A. 12
    B. 13
    C. 15
    D. 14

13. The employee Darden, Kim is listed number ____ on the chronological list of dates hired.
    A. 4
    B. 5
    C. 6
    D. 7

14. The name of the employee whose employee number is listed number 18 on the chronological employee number-list is _____:
    A. Kevaney, Pamela
    B. Brady, Sam
    C. Jameson, Erik
    D. Vawn, George

15. Employee Chin Robert's employee number is listed number ____ on the chronological list of employee numbers.
    A. 10
    B. 13
    C. 11
    D. 12

16. The employee whose employee number is number 10 on the chronological list of employee numbers works in the ____ department.
    A. General Clerk
    B. Special Term
    C. Calendar
    D. Small Claims

17. The employee name that appears as number 12 on the employee list (by department order) is____.
    A. Zoolander, David
    B. Brady, Sam
    C. Ryker, Irma
    D. Williams, Joyce

18. The department which has the greatest number of employees assigned to it is:
    A. Landlord and Tenant
    B. Special Term
    C. Judgments
    D. Small Claims

19. The employee who is listed second in the Landlord and Tenant Department in the employee list (by department order) is:
    A. Brady
    B. Davidson
    C. Young
    D. Chin

CLERICAL ASSISTANT

FILING QUESTION 3

Below is a list of employees, the date each was hired, the employee title, and assignment.

First, prepare 4 lists of the employees in the following order:
1. alphabetical order by last name
2. date hired order
3. title order (and employees within that title in alphabetical order)
4. department assigned order (and alphabetical order of employees in department)

After preparing the above lists, answer the questions that follow.
(You will not be graded on the lists. You will only be graded on how you answer the questions).

NAME	DATE HIRED	TITLE	DEPT. ASSIGNMENT
Minitz, John	6/5/1982	Senior Court Clerk	General Clerk
Beinstein, Laura	6/2/2001	Court Assistant	Special Term
Broafy, Charles	3/6/2001	Law Steno	Landlord and Tenant
Jefferson, Chris	3/4/1987	Court Officer	Security
Anderson, David	2/6/2002	Data Entry Clerk	Small Claims
Waters, Frank	4/1/1996	Analyst	Administration
Holmes, Peter	7/9/1985	Court Office Assistant	General Clerk
Peters, Robert	3/2/1996	Interpreter	Small Claims
Border, Pamela	7/4/1988	Data Entry Clerk	Judgments
Motorson, Vivian	9/4/1998	Law Steno	Special Term
Pacer, John	3/1/1985	Court Officer	Security
Bronson, Vivian	6/17/2004	Senior Court Clerk	Judgments
Johnson, George	7/3/1998	Court Office Assistant	Landlord and Tenant
Clinton, James	5/4/1987	Data Entry Clerk	Small Claims
Porter, Ellen	9/8/1999	Interpreter	Appeals
Abramson, Jill	4/5/1984	Associate Court Clerk	Special Term
Ohler, Wanda	3/9/2001	Analyst	Landlord and Tenant
Olivier, Barry	5/6/1989	Interpreter	Special Term
Dearden, Lucy	5/1/1983	Court Assistant	Calendar
Humes, Eileen	6/6/2002	Court Clerk	Warrants
Reames, Nancy	4/5/1976	Senior Attorney	Special Term
Rister, Irene	4/7/2003	Secretary	Judgments
Zames, Doris	3/2/2003	Interpreter	Landlord and Tenant
Vargas, Louis	6/4/1973	Senior Attorney	Calendar
Davidson, Mark	8/5/1996	Court Assistant	Landlord and Tenant

CLERICAL ASSISTANT

LAST NAME ALPHABETICAL ORDER

y　　　*z*

1. The title of the employee who is number 19 on the alphabetical list of employees is _____.
A. Court Officer   C. Interpreter
B. Court Assistant   D. None of the above

2. The date hired of the employee who is number 11 on the alphabetical list of employees is _____.
A. 3/1/85   C. 6/17/2004
B. 6/6/2002   D. None of the above

3. The employees that are number 13 and 14 on the alphabetical list of employees are _____.
A. Minitz and Motorson
B. Jefferson and Johnson
C. Johnson and Motorson
D. Johnson and Minitz

CLERICAL ASSISTANT

FILING BY DATE HIRED ORDER

4. The employee hired date that is number 14 on the chronological list of employee hired dates is _____.
A. 8/5/96　　C. 7/3/98
B. 4/1/96　　D. None of the above

5. The name of the employee whose hired date is number twelve on the chronological list of employee hired dates is _____.
A. Vivian Bronson　C. Bronson, Vivian
B. Robert Peters　　D. None of the above

6. The title of the employee whose hired date comes directly after the hired date of 7/9/85 on the chronological list of employee hired dates is _____.
A. Court Officer
B. Court Office Assistant
C. Court Assistant
D. None of the above

CLERICAL ASSISTANT

FILING BY TITLE ORDER

7. The second employee listed in the third alphabetical group of employees titles is named _____.
   A. Humes
   B. Bernstein
   C. Davidson
   D. Dearden

8. The 10th employee title listed on the alphabetical list of employee titles is _____.
   A. Law Steno
   B. Secretary
   C. Senior Attorney
   D. Interpreter

9. Which of the following titles has the least number of employees?
   A. Senior Court Clerk
   B. Law Steno
   C. Court Office Assistant
   D. Court Clerk

CLERICAL ASSISTANT

FILING BY ASSIGNMENT

10. Which of the following group of titles has the same number of employees listed?
A. Calendar and Appeals
B. Judgments and Security
C. Small Claims and General Clerk
D. Special Term and Landlord and Tenant

11. Which employee name comes after Pacer on the alphabetical list of employees (by Department)?
A. Anderson
B. Peters
C. Qualms
D. None of the above

12. The employee that is number 7 on the alphabetical list of employees (by department) was hired on _____.
A. 7/9/1985
B. 7/4/1988
C. 3/2/1996
D. None of the above.

CLERICAL ASSISTANT

Answers for Filing Question 3: (Correct answers are in bold and underlined.)

1. The title of the employee who is number 19 on the alphabetical list of employees is:
   A. Court Officer
   B. Court Assistant
   C. Interpreter
   D. None of the above

2. The date hired of the employee who is number 11 on the alphabetical list of employees is:
   A. 3/1/85
   B. 6/6/2002
   C. 6/17/2004
   D. None of the above

3. The employees that are number 13 and 14 on the alphabetical list of employees are:
   A. Minitz and Motorson
   B. Jefferson and Johnson
   C. Johnson and Motorson
   D. Johnson and Minitz

4. The employee hired date that is number 14 on chronological list of employee hired dates is:
   A. 8/5/96
   B. 4/1/96
   C. 7/3/98
   D. None of the above

5. The name of the employee whose hired date is number twelve on the chronological list of employee hired dates is:
   A. Vivian Bronson
   B. Robert Peters
   C. Bronson, Vivian
   D. None of the above

6. The title of the employee whose hired date comes directly after the hired date of 7/9/85 on the chronological list of employee hired dates is:
   A. Court Officer
   B. Court Office Assistant
   C. Court Assistant
   D. None of the above

7. The second employee listed in the third alphabetical group of employees titles is named:
   A. Humes
   B. Bernstein
   C. Davidson
   D. Dearden

8. The 10th employee title listed on the alphabetical list of employee titles is:
   A. Law Steno
   B. Secretary
   C. Senior Attorney
   D. Interpreter

9. Which of the following titles has the least number of employees?
   A. Senior Court Clerk
   B. Law Steno
   C. Court Office Assistant
   D. Court Clerk

10. Which of the following group of titles has the same number of employees listed?
    A. Calendar and Appeals
    B. Judgments and Security
    C. Small Claims and General Clerk
    D. Special Term and Landlord and Tenant

11. Which employee name comes after Pacer on the alphabetical list of employees (by Department)?
    A. Anderson
    B. Peters
    C. Qualms
    D. None of the above

12. The employee that is number 7 on the alphabetical list of employees (by department) was hired on:
    A. 7/9/1985
    B. 7/4/1988
    C. 3/2/1996
    D. None of the above.

CLERICAL ASSISTANT

REMINDER OF HELPFUL TECHNIQUES TO REMEMBER

1. FILING BY ALPHABETICAL ORDER:

Unless instructed otherwise:
1. Alphabetize employee names by their LAST name
   James, John (JAMES is the last name–note the comma after James)
   John James (James is the last name–no comma between the first and last name)
2. Re-write as little information as possible (Just write the LAST names unless there are two or more people with the same last name.)
3. Do NOT re-write unnecessary columns (information about an employee can be obtained from the information provided in the original columns.)
4. After you finish putting a column in order, COUNT the number of names and agree it to the number of names provided to make certain you have not skipped any names.

2. FILING BY DATE HIRED:

Unless instructed otherwise:
1. The OLDEST DATE is listed first (The MOST RECENT DATE is listed last.)
2. When you write a date, try to use the date format "6-5-06" instead of "6/5/06" to avoid confusing the "/" with the number "1".
3. Do NOT re-write unnecessary columns (information about a hire date can be obtained from the information provided in the original columns.)
4. After you finish putting a column in order, COUNT the number of dates and agree it to the number of dates provided to make certain you have not skipped any dates.

3. FILING BY TITLE (and then EMPLOYEE NAME ORDER WITHIN THAT TITLE)

Unless instructed otherwise:
1. List the titles in alphabetical order and **ALSO** list the employees within that title in last name alphabetical order.
2. Re-write as little information as possible (Just write the LAST names unless there are two or more people with the same last name.)
3. Do NOT re-write unnecessary columns (information about an employee in a title can be obtained from the information provided in the original columns.)
4. After you finish putting a column in order, COUNT the number of names and titles and agree them to the number of names provided to make certain you haven't skipped any names or titles.

4. FILING BY ASSIGNMENT
(and then EMPLOYEE NAME ORDER WITHIN THAT ASSIGNMENT)

Use the same techniques as in number "3" above.

CLERICAL ASSISTANT

CLERICAL CHECKING QUESTIONS

3

"These questions measure a candidate's ability to distinguish between sets of names, numbers, letters and/or codes which are almost exactly alike. There are three sets of information which may appear in different fonts. Candidates will be asked to compare the information in the three sets and identify whether the sets differ. Candidates must use the directions provided to determine the correct answer.*

INFORMATION COMPARISON WARM-UP EXERCISE

Example #1:

Kronos Timekeeper Station #3-1893   *Kronos Timekeeper Station #3-1893*

Same or different?

Example #2:

Magnetometer Station # *3-1893*   MAGNETOMETER STATION # *3-1893*

Same or different?   (See page 33 for answers)

Exercise 1:

Below are 5 sets of information (Questions 1-5). For each set of information, compare the information in column 1 and column 2. Blacken "choice A" if the information in both columns is the same. Blacken choice "B" if the information is different in any way.

1. James Bronston
   Employee I.D. # 891724-1
   Civil Court, Kings County

   James Bronston
   Employee I.D. # 897124-1
   Civil Court, Kings County   (A)   (B)

CLERICAL ASSISTANT

1. Kilfoile vs. Karmensky　　　　　Kilfoile vs. Karmensky
　　Cal. Num. 4829/98　　　　　　　Cal. Num. 4829/98
　　Johnson and Wang, P.C.　　　　Johnson and Wang, P.C.　　　　(A)　(B)

3. *Trial date: 3/16/01*　　　　　　Trial date: 3/16/01
　　KCV 251953/99　　　　　　　　　KCV 251953/99
　　Hon. Martin C. Worth　　　　　　Hon. Martin C. Worth
　　Chin, Lieber and Dickenson　　Chin, Leiber and Dickenson　　(A)　(B)

4. C.O. Evelyn Garcia　　　　　　　C.O. Evelyn Garcia
　　Shield Number 71913　　　　　　Shield Number 71913
　　12/20/82 and 3/12/90　　　　　　12/20/82 and 3/12/90
　　Supreme Court, Bronx County　　Supreme Count, Bronx County　(A)　(B)

5. MGM/Mirage Inc.　　　　　　　　*MGM/Mirage, Inc.*
　　Filed: 7-17-01　　　　　　　　　Filed: 7-17-01
　　Emerg. Tel. No. (718) 643-8732　*Emerg. Tel. No. (718) 648-8732*
　　Verdict Date: 12/15/01　　　　　*Verdict Date: 12/15/01*　　　　(A)　(B)

Below are 5 sets of information (Questions 6-10). For each set of information, compare the information in column 1 and column 2. Blacken "choice B" if the information in both columns is the same. Blacken choice "A" if the information is different in any way.

6. Liuni, Worstein and Miara　　　　Liuni, Worstein and Miara
　　Criminal & Family Court Practice　Criminal & Family Court Practice
　　16 Court St. - Suite 1732　　　16 Court St. - Suite 1732
　　Brooklyn, NY 11201-2352　　　　　Brooklyn, NY 11201-2325　　　　(A)　(B)

7. Captain Edward Cornan　　　　　　Captain Edward Cornan
　　Court Officer Jane Liu　　　　　Court Officer Jane Liu
　　Witness: Chales J. Chucko　　　Witness: Chales J. Chucko
　　Inc. Rep. A-7529/01　　　　　　　*Inc. Rep. A-7529/01*　　　　　(A)　(B)

8. Indictment W-79KV　　　　　　　　Indictment W-79KV
　　C. O. Wayne Grumholtz　　　　　C.O. Wayne Grumholts
　　Judge Marlene W. Korres　　　　　Judge Marlene W. Korres
　　Preference (A): 79　　　　　　　　Preference (A): 79　　　　　　(A)　(B)

32

CLERICAL ASSISTANT

9. 79387-295419 Q-V
    Rooms 207, 705, 824, 401
    1/16/01, 2/25/01, 5/15/01
    Barley, C.O. Ferman, C.R.

    79387-295419 Q-V
    Rooms 207, 705, 824, 401
    1/16/01, 2/25/01, 5/15/01
    Barley, C.O. Furman, C.R.   (A)   (B)

10. Code YK-NY-872901
    Section CPLR 325.25 (c)
    Rm. 801 and 809 (a)
    Cal. Num. KCV 28546-01

    Code YK-NY-872901
    Section CPLR 325.25 (c)
    Rm. 801 and 809 (a)
    Cal. Num. KCV 281546-01   (A)   (B)

Answers to Ex. 1 and Ex. 2 (on page 33): Information is the same in both examples. (The fonts are different, but the information is the same.)

Answers 1 - 10

Did you notice that the first question was numbered "1" and that the second question was also numbered "1"?

Errors such as this may appear on any exam. **Don't let such errors make you lose concentration.**

In this case, treat the second question as though it was properly labeled "2" and answer it. In almost all cases, errors will be adjusted later on by the testing authority and **will not affect your score.**

Answers to Exercise 1: (Please note that instructions for questions 1-5 are completely the opposite of instructions for questions 6-10.) Differences in the information are underlined.

1. B Different information: Employee I.D. # 891724-1   Employee I.D. # 897124-1
2. A The information is the same in both columns.
3. B Different information: *Chin, Lieber and Dickenson*   Chin, Leiber and Dickenson
4. B Different information: Supreme Court, Bronx County   Supreme Count, Bronx County
5. B Different information: Emerg. Tel. No. (718) 643-8732   *Emerg. Tel. No. (718) 648-8732*
6. A Different information: Brooklyn, NY 11201-2352   Brooklyn, NY 11201-2325
7. B The information is the same in both columns.
8. A Different information: *C.O. Wayne Grumholtz*   C.O. Wayne Grumholts
9. A Different information: Barley, C.O. Ferman, C.R.   Barley, C.O. Furman, C.R.
10. A Different information: Cal. Num. KCV 28546-01   Cal. Num. KCV 281546-01

CLERICAL ASSISTANT

Please keep in mind the following points:

Question: Does A = *A* ?

Answer: YES !

Also, **A** = *A* = A = A = ▲ = A = **A** ....

1. The instructions for the Warm-Up Exercise ask that you compare the <u>INFORMATION</u> in the two sets. Use of different *fonts* or *typefaces* (the way that the letters are displayed) does NOT change the information. Therefore, according to the instructions, "782 Smith Street" has the identical INFORMATION as *"782 Smith Street"*.

2. If there is an obvious error in the test such as in the Warm-Up Exercise (two "number 1" examples), do not let the error make you lose time or concentration. Make the best of it. Make sure that you answer it the best way that you can. In the above example, treat the first "number 1" as example number 1, and treat the second "number 1" as example number 2. Do not dwell on the error. The fairness of the test undergoes review after the test date. Anything which is incorrect or unfair will probably be adjusted.

3. IF this type of question is **timed** (you are given a specified period of time to answer the questions) work as quickly and accurately as you can so that you will answer all the questions.

If this type of question is **not timed**, or you are given sufficient time to answer the questions AND also go over them, then check and re-check your answers until you are sure that you have answered all the questions accurately and you have not lost any points. Whether timed or not timed, make sure that you answer all the questions.

DO NOT LEAVE ANY ANSWERS BLANK.

You are **NOT** penalized for guessing (as on traditional SAT tests).

4. Pay careful attention to the instructions. In the examples on the following pages, the instructions are more complicated than in the Warm-Up Exercise. (They are more like the test.) Make sure that your answers follow the instructions (<u>-and remember that instructions for these types of questions **may change** two or more times before you have answered all the questions</u>).

CLERICAL ASSISTANT

5. In comparing sets of information, be careful about the following:

    a. inversion of numbers (1452738........1425738)   [the "52" and "25"]

    b. numbers omitted (3452739...............345739)   ["2" is omitted in the second set]

    c. numbers added (823567..................8235967)   [the added "9" in the second set]

    d. letters inverted (Freidrich................Friedrich)   [the "ei" and "ie"]

    e. letters omitted (Smythe......................Smyth)   [the "e"]

    f. letters added (Baskerville.............Baskersville)   [the "s"]

6. If you find one difference in a column, do **NOT** look for more differences (one difference is sufficient).

If you finish the test early (and you have checked all your answers) do **NOT** get up and go home.

If permitted, keep on checking your answers over and over again.

These are questions that you should **NOT** lose one point on.

CLERICAL ASSISTANT

MAKING SURE YOU UNDERSTAND *THE QUESTION*:

Below are examples of directions variations for this type of question. Read the directions carefully. I always made the short notations that you see on the right hand column to make sure that I understood the directions and as a quick reference (to keep the direction choices clear in my mind) as I answered the questions as quickly and carefully as I could.

A. Only the first and third sets are exactly alike.   1=3
B. Only the second and third sets are exactly alike.   2=3
C. All three sets are exactly alike.   =
D. None of the three sets are exactly alike.   X

A. None of the three sets are exactly alike.   X
B. Only the first and third sets are exactly alike.   1=3
C. Only the second and third sets are exactly alike.   2=3
D. All three sets are exactly alike.   =

A. Only the second and third sets are exactly alike.   2=3
B. Only the first and third sets are exactly alike.   1=3
C. None of the sets are exactly alike.   X
D. All three sets are exactly alike.   =

A. Only the second and third sets are exactly alike.   2=3
B. Only the first and second sets are exactly alike.   1=2
C. None of the sets are exactly alike.   X
D. All three sets are exactly alike.   =

A. Only the second and third sets are exactly alike.   2=3
B. Only the first and second sets are exactly alike.   1=2
C. All three sets are exactly alike.   =
D. None of the sets are exactly alike.   X

CLERICAL ASSISTANT

Exercise 2 (10 questions):

Directions: For questions 1-5 below, compare the three sets of information and mark your answer sheet with the correct choice, as follows:

A. Only the first and third sets are exactly alike.
B. Only the second and third sets are exactly alike.
C. All three sets are exactly alike.
D. None of the three sets are exactly alike.

1. James Ellmore
   8468 Ulysses Ave.
   NY Supreme Ct.
   E-67298034-8762
   Epcot & Elderts P.C.

   James Ellmore
   8468 Ulysses Ave.
   NY Supreme Ct.
   E-67298043-8762
   Epcot & Elderts P.C.

   James Ellmore
   8468 Ulysses Ave.
   NY Supreme Ct.
   E-67298034-8762
   Epcot & Elderts P.C.

2. TXS-932820384
   Rosweig, Jimenez
   SPT Svcs., Inc.
   7/09/01 (247132)
   CPLR, Section 739

   TXS-932820384
   Roswieg, Jimenez
   SPT Svcs., Inc.
   7/09/01 (247132)
   CPLR, Section 739

   TXS-932820384
   Rosweig, Jimenez
   SPT Svcs., Inc.
   7/09/01 (247132)
   CPLR, Section 739

3. Whoenig, Francois
   E#: 50692/01
   I.D. No. 3967298-9
   Queens, NY 11335
   719-17 235th Street

   Whoenig, Francois
   E#: 50692/01
   I.D. No. 3967298-9
   Queens, NY 11335
   719-17 235th Street

   Whoenig, Francois
   E#: 50692/01
   I.D. No. 3967298-9
   Queens, NY 11335
   719-17 235th Street

4. Greenstein & Wong
   Fed. ID #: 563298-75
   293 Sycamore Dr. (E)
   068-39-7932

   Greenstein & Wong
   Fed. ID #: 5631298-75
   293 Sycamore Dr. (E)
   068-39-7932

   Greenstein & Wong
   Fed. ID #: 563298-75
   293 Sycamore Dr. (E)
   068-39-7923

5. Mr. Jacki Lee-Jones
   6719 Ft. Gant Ave.
   S. Richmond Terrace
   R Date: 12/21/02
   Ref. No. 5264-9842

   Ms. Jacki Lee-Jones
   6719 Ft. Gant Ave.
   S. Richmond Terrace
   R Date: 12/21/02
   Ref. No. 5264-9842

   Ms. Jacki Lee-Jones
   6719 Ft. Gant Ave.
   S. Richmond Terrace
   R Date: 12/21/02
   Ref. No. 5264-9842

CLERICAL ASSISTANT

Directions: For questions 6-10 below, compare the three sets of information and mark your answer sheet with the correct choice, as follows:

A. None of the three sets are exactly alike.
B. Only the first and third sets are exactly alike.
C. Only the second and third sets are exactly alike.
D. All three sets are exactly alike.

6. CFK837652951
   CIV-5632/01
   New Jersey, 1998
   NYU Law School
   J. Kay F. Lee

   CFK837652951
   New Jersey, 1998
   CIV-5632/01
   J. Kay F. Lee
   NYU Law School

   CFK837652951
   NYU Law School
   J. Kay F. Lee
   CIV-5632/01
   New Jersey, 1998

7. C.O. H. Bachert
   Judge K.J. Brendan
   C.R. Steve Shapiro
   O.C.R. Jose Rosario
   V.P. Ed Lorenzini

   C.R. Steve Shapiro
   O.C.R. Jose Rosario
   V.P. Ed Lorenzini
   Judge K.J. Brendun
   C.O. H. Bachert

   V.P. Ed Lorenzini
   Judge K.J. Brandan
   C.O. H. Bachert
   C.R. Steve Shapiro
   O.C.R. Jose Rosario

8. Telemaro, Maxine
   FCA(213); CPL(1037)
   245 Adams St., 2 fl.
   25 to Life (J. Burns)
   Evid. #17A-1 (Photo)

   245 Adams St., 2 fl.
   25 to Life (J. Burns)
   Evid. #17A-1 (Photo)
   FCA(213); CPL(1037)
   Telemarco, Maxine

   FCA(213);CPL(1037)
   Evid. #17A-1 (Photo)
   Telemaro, Maxine
   245 Adams St., 2 fl.
   25 to Life (J. Burns)

9. Kim R. Wong
   SS#: 127-78-8392
   79-728 Venor Drive
   Bronx, NY 10477
   PO Box 29001-65

   79-728 Venor Drive
   Bronx, NY 10477
   Kim R. Wong
   SS#: 127-78-8392
   PO Box 29001-65

   SS#: 127-78-8392
   PO Box 29001-65
   Bronx, NY 10477
   79-728 Venor Drive
   Kim R. Wong

10. NCV 1273192/99
    NYC Crim. Ct.
    Part 19F, Room 1302
    December 20, 1999
    (718) 729-72987

    NYC Crim. Ct.
    NCV 127392/99
    December 20, 1999
    (718) 729-72987
    Part 19F, Room 1302

    Part 19F, Room 1302
    December 20, 1999
    (718) 729-72987
    NCV 127392/99
    NYC Crim. Ct.

Answers for Exercise 2 (1-10):

1. A   2. A   3. C   4. D   5. B   6. D   7. A   8. B   9. D   10. C

(See next two pages for the differences in the sets of information.)

CLERICAL ASSISTANT

Explanatory Answers for Exercise 2: (Differences are in **<u>bold and underlined</u>**.)

Directions: For questions 1-5 below, compare the three sets of information and mark your answer sheet with the correct choice, as follows:

A. Only the first and third sets are exactly alike.
B. Only the second and third sets are exactly alike.
C. All three sets are exactly alike.
D. None of the three sets are exactly alike.

<u>**Answers**</u>

1. James Ellmore
   8468 Ulysses Ave.
   NY Supreme Ct.
   E-67298**<u>034</u>**-8762
   Epcot & Elderts P.C.

   James Ellmore
   8468 Ulysses Ave.
   NY Supreme Ct.
   E-67298**<u>043</u>**-8762
   Epcot & Elderts P.C.

   James Ellmore
   8468 Ulysses Ave.
   NY Supreme Ct.
   E-67298**<u>034</u>**-8762
   Epcot & Elderts P.C.

   <u>A</u>

2. TXS-932820384
   <u>Rosweig</u>, Jimenez
   SPT Svcs., Inc.
   7/09/01 (247132)
   CPLR, Section 739

   TXS-932820384
   <u>Rosweig</u>, Jimenez
   SPT Svcs., Inc.
   7/09/01 (247132)
   CPLR, Section 739

   TXS-932820384
   <u>Rosweig</u>, Jimenez
   SPT Svcs., Inc.
   7/09/01 (247132)
   CPLR, Section 739

   <u>A</u>

3. Whoenig, Francois
   E#: 50692/01
   I.D. No. 3967298-9
   Queens, NY 11335
   719-17 235th Street

   Whoenig, Francois
   E#: 50692/01
   I.D. No. 3967298-9
   Queens, NY 11335
   719-17 235th Street

   Whoenig, Francois
   E#: 50692/01
   I.D. No. 3967298-9
   Queens, NY 11335
   719-17 235th Street

   <u>C</u>

4. Greenstein & Wong
   Fed. ID #: **<u>563298</u>**-75
   293 Sycamore Dr. (E)
   068-39-**<u>7932</u>**

   Greenstein & Wong
   Fed. ID #: **<u>5631298</u>**-75
   293 Sycamore Dr. (E)
   068-39-**<u>7932</u>**

   Greenstein & Wong
   Fed. ID #: **<u>563298</u>**-75
   293 Sycamore Dr. (E)
   068-39-**<u>7923</u>**

   <u>D</u>

5. **<u>Mr.</u>** Jacki Lee-Jones
   6719 Ft. Gant Ave.
   S. Richmond Terrace
   R Date: 12/21/02
   Ref. No. 5264-9842

   <u>Ms.</u> Jacki Lee-Jones
   6719 Ft. Gant Ave.
   S. Richmond Terrace
   R Date: 12/21/02
   Ref. No. 5264-9842

   <u>Ms.</u> Jacki Lee-Jones
   6719 Ft. Gant Ave.
   S. Richmond Terrace
   R Date: 12/21/02
   Ref. No. 5264-9842

   <u>B</u>

CLERICAL ASSISTANT

Directions: For questions 6-10 below, compare the three sets of information and mark your answer sheet with the correct choice, as follows:

A. None of the three sets are exactly alike.
B. Only the first and third sets are exactly alike.
C. Only the second and third sets are exactly alike.
D. All three sets are exactly alike.

Answers

6. CFK837652951 CIV-5632/01 New Jersey, 1998 NYU Law School J. Kay F. Lee	CFK837652951 New Jersey, 1998 CIV-5632/01 J. Kay F. Lee NYU Law School	CFK837652951 NYU Law School J. Kay F. Lee CIV-5632/01 New Jersey, 1998	**D**
7. C.O. H. Bachert Judge K.J. **Brendan** C.R. Steve Shapiro O.C.R. Jose Rosario V.P. Ed Lorenzini	C.R. Steve Shapiro O.C.R. Jose Rosario V.P. Ed Lorenzini Judge K.J. **Brendun** C.O. H. Bachert	V.P. Ed Lorenzini Judge K.J. **Brandan** C.O. H. Bachert C.R. Steve Shapiro O.C.R. Jose Rosario	**A**
8. **Telemaro,** Maxine FCA(213); CPL(1037) 245 Adams St., 2 fl. 25 to Life (J. Burns) Evid. #17A-1 (Photo)	245 Adams St., 2 fl. 25 to Life (J. Burns) Evid. #17A-1 (Photo) FCA(213); CPL(1037) **Telemarco,** Maxine	FCA(213);CPL(1037) Evid. #17A-1 (Photo) **Telemaro,** Maxine 245 Adams St., 2 fl. 25 to Life (J. Burns)	**B**
9. Kim R. Wong SS#: 127-78-8392 79-728 Venor Drive Bronx, NY 10477 PO Box 29001-65	79-728 Venor Drive Bronx, NY 10477 Kim R. Wong SS#: 127-78-8392 PO Box 29001-65	SS#: 127-78-8392 PO Box 29001-65 Bronx, NY 10477 79-728 Venor Drive Kim R. Wong	**D**
10. NCV **1273192**/99 NYC Crim. Ct. Part 19F, Room 1302 December 20, 1999 (718) 729-72987	NYC Crim. Ct. NCV **127392**/99 December 20, 1999 (718) 729-72987 Part 19F, Room 1302	Part 19F, Room 1302 December 20, 1999 (718) 729-72987 NCV **127392**/99 NYC Crim. Ct.	**C**

CLERICAL ASSISTANT

Exercise 3 (10 questions):

Directions:
For questions 1-5 below, compare the three sets of information and mark your answer sheet with the correct choice, as follows:

A. Only the first and third sets are exactly alike.
B. Only the second and third sets are exactly alike.
C. All three sets are exactly alike.
D. None of the three sets are exactly alike.

1. *ACC Emore Lubor*
   Family Court - SI
   782 Castington St.
   LT 265481/1998
   Line No. 659872786

   ACC Emor Lubor
   Family Court - SI
   782 Castington St.
   LT 265481/1998
   Line No. 659872786

   ACC Emore Lubor
   Family Court - SI
   782 Castington St.
   LT 265481/1998
   Line No. 659872786

2. **Carmen Saronya-Lee**
   C.O. Sam Lumeria
   Police Rep. # B-8291
   Friday, 10:37 AM
   Entrance A (6-7 fls.)

   Carmen Saronya-Lee
   C.O. Sam Lumeria
   Police Rep. # B-8291
   Friday, 10:37 AM
   Entrance A (6-7 fl.)

   Carmen Saronya-Lee
   C.O. Sam Lumeria
   Police Rep. # B-8291
   Friday, 10:37 AM
   Entrance A (6-7 fl.)

3. *9:00 AM - 9:35 AM*
   Damien, Oswego
   T-7295639838
   FC399827.62876C
   Kings Records Dept.

   9:00 AM - 9:35 AM
   Damien, Oswego
   T-7295639838
   FC399827.62876C
   Kings Records Dept.

   9:00 AM - 9:35 AM
   Damien, Oswego
   T-7295639838
   FC399827.62876C
   Kings Records Dept.

4. Bodton - Reiker Inc.
   Sr. Court Attorney 31
   Crim. Proc. Law 256
   Bodiker, Robert
   BXC739556289

   Bodton - Rieker Inc.
   Sr. Court Attorney 31
   Crim. Proc. Law 526
   Bodiker, Robert
   BXC739556289

   Bodton - Rieker Inc.
   Sr. Court Attorney 13
   Crim. Proc. Law 256
   Bodiker, Robert
   BXC739556289

5. Loumas,Edward
   A&R Process Serving
   NCR2648-7819

   Loumas,Edward
   A&R Process Serving
   NCR2648-7819

   Loumas,Edward
   A&R Process Serving
   NCR2648-7819

CLERICAL ASSISTANT

Directions:
For questions 6-10 below, compare the three sets of information and mark your answer sheet with the correct choice, as follows:

A. None of the three sets are exactly alike.
B. Only the first and third sets are exactly alike.
C. Only the second and third sets are exactly alike.
D. All three sets are exactly alike.

6. Front Entrance 11B
   Magnetometer 798-H
   Inspector K. Wolfson
   Police Rep. #U-3728

   Magnetometer 798-H
   Front Entrance 11B
   Police Rep. #U-3728
   Inspector K. Wolfson

   Police Rep. #U-3728
   Inspector K. Wolfson
   Magnetometer 798-H
   Front Entrance 11B

7. 1793 Leonard St.
   H97-826532CVD
   Parkers Labs Inc.
   Suffolk Cty. 17623

   Parkers Labs Inc.
   1793 Lenard St.
   Suffolk Cty. 17623
   H97-826532CVD

   1793 Leonard St.
   Parkers Labs Inc.
   H97-826532CVD
   Suffolk Cty. 17623

8. LawH0391231372
   J. Hektor Ayub, Sr.
   Miranda, Victoria
   LIC-28 (1999-25)

   Miranda, Victoria
   LIC-28 (1999-25)
   J. Hector Ayub, Sr.
   LawH0391231372

   LIC-28 (1999-25)
   LawH0391231372
   Miranda, Victoria
   J. Hector Ayub, Sr.

9. NCS962898-6372
   Mohammud Alumar
   Priority CD/281724
   ST Bronx Invest., Inc.

   Priority CD/281724
   ST Bronx Invest., Inc.
   Mohammed Alumar
   NCS962898-6372

   NCS962898-6372
   ST Bronx Invest., Inc.
   Priority CD/281724
   Mohammed Alumar

10. Bellaggio, Las Vegas
    Theft of $27,575.12
    Damage S2673
    KCV 281765/98

    Damage S2673
    KCV 281765/89
    Bellaggio, Las Vegas
    Theft of $27,575.12

    KCV 281765/98
    Theft of $27,575.12
    Damage S2673
    Bellaggio, Las Vegas

Answers for Exercise 3 (1-10) are at the top of the following page.

CLERICAL ASSISTANT

Answers for Exercise 3 (Questions 1-10) on the preceding pages are:

1. A
2. B
3. C
4. D
5. C

6. D
7. B
8. C
9. C
10. B

Exercise 4:

Directions:

For questions 1- 4 below, compare the three sets of information and mark your answer sheet with the correct choice, as follows:

A. Only the first and third sets are exactly alike.
B. Only the second and third sets are exactly alike.
C. All three sets are exactly alike.
D. None of the three sets are exactly alike.

1. George R. Walsh
SS#: 872-78-7191
Tsf. Req. - Bronx
CO74397183424
NYC FC 7/24/94

    George R. Walsh
    SS#: 872-78-7191
    Tsf. Req. - Bronx
    CO74397183424
    NYC FC 1/24/94

    George R. Walsh
    SS#: 872-78-7191
    Tsf. Req. - Bronx
    CO74397183424
    NYC FC 7/24/94

2. DERIK AHMUD, JR.
175-72 Elmont Ave.
PO Box 28563829
Batavia, NY 16294

    PO Box 28563829
    Batavia, NY 16294
    175-72 Elmont Ave.
    Derik Ahmud, Jr.

    Batavia, NY 16294
    Derik Ahmud, Jr.
    PO Box 28563829
    175-72 Elmont Ave.

3. PCC FRED NYUEN
19th floor - rm 1978
NYK 1937176/01
Proc. 276548719-17

    NYK 1937176/01
    Proc. 27654879-17
    PCC Fred Nyuen
    19th floor - rm 1978

    Proc. 27654879-17
    PCC Fred Nyuen
    19th floor - rm 1978
    NYK 1937176/01

4. **Ms. Renee Sinatra**
Police Rep. # SX B-3
Friday, 12:56 PM
CCN-01-3428918/01

    Friday, 12:56 PM
    CCN-01-342898/01
    Police Rep. # SX B-3
    Ms. Renee Sinatra

    Police Rep. # SX B-3
    CCN-01-3428918/01
    Ms. Renee Sinatra
    Friday, 12:56 PM

CLERICAL ASSISTANT

Directions:

For questions 5-10 below, compare the three sets of information and mark your answer sheet with the correct choice, as follows:

A. None of the three sets are exactly alike.
B. Only the first and third sets are exactly alike.
C. Only the second and third sets are exactly alike.
D. All three sets are exactly alike.

5. Stairwell A (Rm. 701)
Inspector H. Atiles
Part 18G (J. Ferrar)
Inc. AB/1999-2001)
December 18, 2000

Stairwell A (Rm. 701)
Inspector H. Atiles
Part 18G (J. Ferrar)
Inc. AB/1999-2001)
December 18, 2000

Stairwell A (Rm. 701)
Inspector H. Atiles
Part 18G (J. Ferrar)
Inc. AB/1999-2001)
December 18, 2000

6. KFH7382765016
Morris, Eleonore
Priority List G-276
J. Peterson, Patricia

J. Peterson, Patricia
KFH7382765016
Morris, Elenore
Priority List G-276

Priority List G-276
Morris, Eleonore
KFH7382765016
J. Peterson, Patricia

7. **SCK 37629/1999**
Wolfbard vs. Yungs
Wed. Jan. 12, 2002
6:30 PM, Rm. 305
Adjourned Motions

SCK 37629/1999
Wolfbard vs. Youngs
Wed. Jan. 12, 2002
Adjourned Motions
6:30 PM, Rm. 305

Wolfbard vs. Youngs
SCK 37629/1999
Wed. Jan. 12, 2002
Adjourned Motions
6:30 PM, Rm. 305

8. Turnober, Matthew
FC, CIV & FCA
Reg. 96753876592
KV38765.2987-1

Reg. 96753876592
KV38765.2987-1
FC, CIV & FCA
Turnober, Matthew

KV38765.2987-1
Reg. 96753876592
FC, CIV & FCA
Turnober, Matthew

9. **SCC Oliver Wosinsky**
Capt. Reynolds Wood
Thursday, June 26-02
Inspector R. Urango
Entrance B (1 fl.)

SCC Oliver Wozinsky
Capt. Reynolds Wood
Thursday, June 26-02
Inspector R. Urango
Entrance B (1 fl.)

SCC Oliver Wosinsky
Capt. Reynolds Wood
Thursday, June 26-02
Inspector R. Urango
Entrance B (1 fl.)

10. Alberta T. Quong
Xaveria R. Muldorf
Dersonig, Bertha
Cass 28/754639-01

Dersonig, Bertha
Cass 28/754639-01
Xaveria R. Mulldorf
Alberta T. Quong

Dersonig, Bertha
Cass 28/754639-01
Alberta T. Quong
Xaveria R. Muldorf

Answers for 1-10 are on the following page.

CLERICAL ASSISTANT

Answers for Exercise 4 (Questions 1-10):

1. A
2. C
3. B
4. A
5. D
6. B
7. C
8. D
9. B
10. B

Sample 5 Exercise:

Directions: For questions 1-10 below, compare the three sets of information and mark your answer sheet with the correct choice, as follows:

A. Only the second and third sets are exactly alike.
B. Only the first and third sets are exactly alike.
C. None of the sets are exactly alike.
D. All three sets are exactly alike.

1. Barry Swathmore
SS#: 63-38-1467
275-20 Whitmore St.
Brooklyn, NY 11201
PO Box 38732

    Barry Swathmore
SS#: 63-38-1467
275-20 Whitmore St.
Brooklyn, NY 11201
PO Box 38732

    Barry Swathmore
SS#: 63-38-1467
275-20 Whitmore St.
Brooklyn, NY 11201
PO Box 38732

2. Cynthia N. Blake
5684 Fennimore Dr.
Staten Island, NY
ID No: 2479145-6
H Date: 12/25/98

    Cynthia N. Blake
5684 Fennimore Dr.
Staten Island, NY
ID No: 2479145-6
H Date: 12/25/89

    Cynthia N. Blake
5684 Fennimore Dr.
Staten Island, NY
ID No: 2479145-6
H Date: 12/25/98

3. Freemont Ind., Inc.
Fed. ID #: 11717117
Frederick Gates, Pres.
263 Lincoln Street
Brookdale, NY

    Freemont Ind., Inc.
Fed. ID #: 11717117
Frederick Gates, Pres.
263 Lincoln Ave.
Brookdale, NY

    Freedmont Ind., Inc.
Fed. ID #: 11717117
Frederick Gates, Pres.
263 Lincoln Street
Brookvale, NY

4. Mr. Ellmore Grant, Sr.
Rockville Centre Div.
2786 Lakeview Rd.
Ref. No 2546-8924
1/16/98 - 2/26/99

    Mr. Ellmore Grant, Sr.
Rockville Centre Div.
2786 Lakeview Rd.
Ref. No 2564-8924
1/16/98 - 2/26/99

    Mr. Ellmore Grant, Sr.
Rockville Centre Div.
2786 Lakeview Rd.
Ref. No 2564-8924
1/16/98 - 2/26/99

CLERICAL ASSISTANT

5. ID No. 064-6739
1729 Ft. Hamilton St.
Staten Island, NY
4-52-89124
S Code: 05692

ID No. 064-6739
1729 St. Hamilton St.
Staten Island, NY
4-52-89124
S Code: 05692

ID No. 064-6739
1729 Ft. Hamilton St.
Staten Island, NY
4-52-89124
S Code: 05692

6. 5827 Batchelder Dr.
Apt. 2A, Left Wing
Priority 7F (NF)
052-69-1729
Alvin Winniper

5827 Batchelder Dr.
Apt. 2A, Left Wing
Priority 7F (NF)
052-69-1792
Alvin Winniper

5827 Batchelder Dr.
Apt. 2A, Left Wing
Priority 7F (NF)
052-69-1729
Alvin Winiper

7. James Ovington, Jr.
250-76-6726
Sept. 13, 2001
Priority 8C-24D
Conf. 78410

James Ovington, Jr.
250-76-6726
Sept. 13, 2001
Priority 8C-24D
Conf. 78410

James Ovington, Jr.
250-76-6726
Sept. 13, 2001
Priority 8C-24D
Conf. 78410

8. C.O. Meredith James
Kings Civil Court
141 Livingston Street
Brooklyn, NY 11201
Part 18E, Room 308

C.O. Meredith James
Kings Civil Court
141 Livingston Street
Brooklyn, NY 11201
Part 18F, Room 308

C.O. Meredith Jones
Kings Civil Court
141 Livingston Street
Brooklyn, NY 11201
Part 18E, Room 308

9. Capt. Mary Rodriguez
Sgt. Edward Johnson
C.O. Eric Dunbar
December 20, 1982
2/15/99 - 3/27/99

Capt. Mary Rodriguez
Sgt. Edward Johnson
C.O. Erik Dunbar
December 20, 1982
2/15/99 - 3/27/99

Capt. Mary Rodriguez
Sgt. Edward Johnson
C.O. Erik Dunbar
December 20, 1982
2/15/99 - 3/27/99

10. Mr. & Mrs. David Tye
174 New Utrecth Ave.
C.O. Friedman
Tel: (718) 682-8395
June 28, 2001

Mr. & Mrs. David Tye
174 New Utrecth Ave.
C.O. Friedman
Tel: (718) 682-8395
June 28, 2001

Mr. & Mrs. David Tye
174 New Utrecth Ave.
C.O. Friedman
Tel: (718) 682-8395
June 28, 2001

The answers for questions 1 - 10 of the Sample 5 Exercise can be found at the top of the following page.

CLERICAL ASSISTANT

Answers for Sample 5 Exercise questions 1 - 10 on the preceding pages are:

1. D
2. B
3. C
4. A
5. B
6. C
7. D
8. C
9. A
10. D

Exercise 6:

Directions: For questions 1 -10, compare the three sets of information and mark your answer sheet with the correct choice, as follows:

A. Only the first and second set are exactly alike.
B. None of the sets are exactly alike.
C. Only the second and third sets are exactly alike.
D. All three sets are exactly alike.

1. SCC Barry Nyue
   Criminal Court - NY
   100 Centre Street
   17th fl. - Rm 1728
   Line No. 873802

   17th fl. - Rm 1728
   100 Centre Street
   Line No. 873802
   SCC Barry Nyue
   Criminal Court - NY

   Line No. 873802
   SCC Barry Nyue
   17th fl. - Rm 1728
   Criminal Court - NY
   100 Centre Street

2. 8:00 AM - 8:45 PM
   Capt. William Rhodes
   Back entrance 7-H
   Magnetometer 1793
   C.O. Henrietta Smythe

   C.O. Henrietta Smythe
   Magnetometer 1793
   8:00 AM - 8:45 PM
   Back entrance 7-H
   Capt. William Rhodes

   Back entrance 7-H
   C.O. Henrietta Smythe
   Capt. William Rhodes
   Magnetometer 1793
   8:00 AM - 8:45 PM

3. SCK 10538/1999
   Davidson vs. Larley
   Thursday, June 26, 2000
   6:30 PM, Room 305
   Adjourned Motion Cal.

   6:30 PM, Room 305
   Adjourned Motion Cal.
   SCK 10538/1999
   Davidson vs. Larley
   Thursday, June 29, 2000

   Davidson vs. Larley
   Thursday, June 26, 2000
   6:30 PM, Room 503
   Adjourned Motion Cal.
   SCK 10538/1999

4. Francois Atejak
   LT 121683/1998
   1798 McDonough St.
   Inspector J. Firley
   Part 18K (J. Brenson)

   Inspector J. Firley
   LT 121683/1998
   Francois Atejak
   1789 McDonough St.
   Part 18K (J. Brenson)

   LT 121683/1998
   Inspector J. Firley
   Part 18K (J. Brenson)
   Francois Atejak
   1789 McDonough St.

47

CLERICAL ASSISTANT

5. Ms. Lois Saronya C.O. Peter Nyguyen Police Rep. # A-2876 **Thursday, 8:29 AM** Stairwell B (4 - 5 fl.)	Police Rep. # A-2876 Thursday, 8:29 AM Stairwell B (4 - 5 fl.) Ms. Lois Saronya C.O. Peter Nyguyen	Stairwell B (4 - 5 fl.) Ms. Lois Saronya Thursday, 8:29 AM C.O. Peter Nyguyen **Police Rep. # A-2876**
6. Ct. Att. Brenda Myers Judge Diana Ovideva (718) 643 - 8207 Ext. 1579 Evers & Backers, Inc.	(718) 643 - 8207 Ext. 1579 Ct. Att. Brenda Myers Evers & Backers, Inc. Judge Diana Ovideva	Ext. 1579 Evers & Backers, Inc. (718) 643 - 8207 Judge Diana Ovideva **Ct. Att. Brenda Myers**
7. C.O. James Bantor County: Richmond Feb. 26, 1998 EN: 506709 Tier 4, (5489210)	Feb. 26, 1998 EN: 506709 Tier 4, (5489210) **C.O. James Bantor** County: Richmond	County: Richmond Feb. 26, 1998 EN: 509709 Tier 4, (5489210) C.O. James Bantor
8. Supreme Court-Queens **Justice Arnold Comper** Capt. William Nowles Chief Clerk Carol Sawyer C.O. Anne Liu	C.O. Anne Liu Chief Clerk Carol Sawyer Capt. William Nowles Justice Arnold Comper Supreme Court-Queens	Supreme Court-Queens Justice Arnold Comper C.O. Anne Lui Chief Clerk Carol Sawyer Capt. William Nowles
9. Security: 10/24/2001 Lobby: 10/28/2001 Office: 11/16/2001 Pt. 12: 12/19/2001 Vac. 12/22/2001	Vac. 12/22/2001 Pt. 21: 12/19/2001 **Security: 10/24/2001** Office: 11/16/2001 Lobby: 10/28/2001	Office: 11/16/2001 Lobby: 10/28/2001 Vac. 12/22/2001 Pt. 12: 12/10/2001 Security: 10/24/2001
10. Susan Joseph, 1642 Albert Smythe, 2793 Peter Yee, 2162 Maria Alvarez, 1124 Diane Cycheck, 1820	Maria Alvarez, 1124 Diane Cycheck, 1820 **Albert Smythe, 2793** Susan Joseph, 1642 Peter Yee, 2162	Peter Yee, 2162 Maria Alvarez, 1124 Diane Cycheck, 1820 Albert Smythe, 2793 Susan Joseph, 1642

Answers for questions 1 – 10 of the Sample 6 Exercise:

1. D
2. D
3. B
4. C
5. D
6. D
7. A
8. A
9. B
10. D

CLERICAL ASSISTANT

COURT RECORD KEEPING QUESTIONS

4

These questions assess candidates' ability to read, combine, and manipulate written information organized from several sources.

Candidates will be presented with different types of tables, which contain names, numbers, codes and other information, and must combine and organize the information to answer specific questions.*

CLERICAL ASSISTANT

COURT RECORD KEEPING TABLES

Understanding Tables

TABLE 1: Criminal Cases Tried During The Week of 2/7/15 - 2/11/15

	Part 2	Part 3	Part 6	Part 7	Part 9	Part 10	Total
Mon 2/7	C	--ROW ROW ROW ROW ROW ROW ROW--------------------
Tues 2/8	O						
Wed 2/9	L						
Thurs 2/10	U						
Fri 2/11	M						
Total	N						(T)

A table consists of columns and rows. Rows go across. Columns go up and down. Each column is labeled on top. Each row is labeled at the left. IF THE TABLE HAS A "TOTAL" FOR THE ROWS AND COLUMNS, the grand total of the "Total" row and "Total" column **(T)** are always equal.

TABLE 2: Criminal Cases Tried During The Week of 2/7/15 - 2/11/15

	Part 2	Part 3	Part 6	Part 7	Part 9	Part 10	Total
Mon 2/7	2	1	3	1	1	2	10
Tues 2/8	3	2	2	2	3	1	13
Wed 2/9	2	1	1	1	3	2	10
Thurs 2/10	1	1	3	2	1	1	9
Fri 2/11	2	3	2	2	3	2	14
Total	10	8	11	8	11	8	56

In TABLE 2 the number of cases tried information for the week is filled out.

Questions:

1. How would we learn how many cases Part 7 had on Thursday? (We look at the Part 7 column and go down until we reach the row (Thursday) that intersects with that column....The answer is 2 cases.)

2. What is the total number of cases tried in Part 6 for the week? (11)

3. What is the total number of cases in all Parts tried on Wednesday? (10)

4. What is the total number of cases tried by Part 3 and Part 9 for the week? (8 + 11 = 19)

5. What is the total number of cases tried by all Parts for the week? (56)

CLERICAL ASSISTANT

The following table provides an exercise on how to fill-in missing information in a table.

TABLE 3: Criminal Cases Tried During The Week of 2/7/15 - 2/11/15

	Part 2	Part 3	Part 6	Part 7	Part 9	Part 10	Total
Mon 2/7	2	1	3	1	1	2	10
Tues 2/8	3		2	2	3	1	13
Wed 2/9	2	1	1	1	3	2	
Thurs 2/10	1	1	3	2	1	1	9
Fri 2/11	2	3	2	2	3	2	14
Total		8	11	8	11	8	

1. What is the total number of cases tried by Part 2 for the week? (2+3+2+1+2=10)
2. How many cases were tried by Part 3 on Tuesday? (8-3-1-1-1=2) or (8-6=2)
3. What is the total number of cases tried on Wednesday? (2+1+1+1+3+2=10)
4. What is the total number of cases tried in all Parts for the week? (Total of rows or columns. Both totals are 56)

TABLE 4: Criminal Cases Tried On Mon. 2/7/2015

Case Number	Part 2	Part 3	Part 6	Part 7	Part 9	Part 10	Jury Trial YES	NO
C48734 -		1					Y	
C48735 -				1				N
C48736 -	1						Y	
C48737			1				Y	
C48738					1			N
C48739						1	Y	
C48740				1				N
C48741					1			N
C48742		1					Y	
C48743			1					N
Total	1	2	2	2	2	1	5	5

Question: How many jury and non jury trials did each Part (courtroom) have on Monday?

(For the exam's much more complex questions, we will need to create and fill out a table, as follows:)

TABLE 5 - Summary Table: Jury and Non Jury Cases Tried By Each Part On 2/7/15

	Part 2	Part 3	Part 6	Part 7	Part 9	Part 10
JURY						
NON JURY						

CLERICAL ASSISTANT

THE FOLLOWING IS A SUGGESTED PROCEDURE FOR FILLING-OUT HELPFUL "SUPPLEMENTARY TABLES" THAT YOU CREATE TO HELP YOU ANSWER THE QUESTIONS.

On the actual test the tables will be much longer.

To save a great amount of time, we will go down each row of the main table (TABLE 4: Criminal Cases Tried On Mon. 2/7/2015) **ONCE ONLY FOR EACH ROW** and capture (post) the information to the supplementary table, as shown below.
The "/" (tick-mark) indicates a case that we have posted from the main table (TABLE 4: Criminal Cases Tried On Mon. 2/7/2015.)

Follow these steps:
Row 1 (Case Number C48734) was tried in Part 3 with a Jury Trial.
We post this in the supplementary table that we created, (TABLE 5 - Summary Table: Jury and Non Jury Cases Tried By Each Part On 2/7/15) by writing a "/" in the Part 3 column, JURY box.
To make sure that we do not post this line again or lose our place, we write a "-" after the case number, C48734.

Row 2 (Case Number C48735) was tried in Part 7 and did NOT have a jury trial.
We post this in the supplementary table that we created, (TABLE 5 - Summary Table: Jury and Non Jury Cases Tried By Each Part On 2/7/15) by writing a "/" in the Part 3 column, NON JURY box.
To make sure that we do not post this line again or lose our place, we write a "-" after the case number, C48735.

Row 3 (Case Number C48736) was tried in Part 2 with a jury trial.
We post this in the supplementary table that we created, (TABLE 5 - Summary Table: Jury and Non Jury Cases Tried By Each Part On 2/7/15) by writing a "/" in the Part 2 column, JURY box.
To make sure that we do not post this line again or lose our place, we write a "-" after the case number, C48736.

We continue doing this for each row. When we have posted all the information, Table 5 should have all the "/" marks as in the illustration below. **On the test there will be a large number of "/" marks, so for clarity we count the number of "/" marks in each box in the table and write the total number of "/" marks in the same box as the "/" marks.**

TABLE 5 - Summary Table: Jury and Non Jury Cases Tried By Each Part On 2/7/15

	Part 2	Part 3	Part 6	Part 7	Part 9	Part 10
JURY	1 /	2 //	1 /			1 /
NON JURY			1 /	2 //	2 //	

A question such as "How many non-jury trials did Part 7 have?" can be answered very quickly by looking at the supplementary Table 5, Part 7 column, Non JURY row. (Answer is "2".)

CLERICAL ASSISTANT

Determining The Missing Case Numbers In A Column Listing Cases In Sequential Order

Part of the table question involves determining and filling-in missing case numbers or other information within the table. In this exercise we will practice how to determine a missing case number from a list of cases in a LOGICAL AND CONSISTENT ORDER. Below are six pairs of lists (A1 through E2). The first column in each pair of lists is a complete list with no gaps (It has the answers for column 2). <u>The second column is the same as the first column, except that it has some blanks to be filled in, as may appear on the table questions on the exam.</u>

A1	A2	B1	B2	C1	C2	D1	D2	E1	E2
1	1	A1	A1	A1	A1	A601	A601	A3601	A3601
2	2	A2	A2	A2	A2	A602	A602	A3602	A3602
3	3	A3	A3	A3	A__?	A603	A603	A3603	___?
4	4	A4	A4	A4	A4	A604	___?	A3604	A3604
5	5	A5	A5	C1	C1	C831	C831	C7831	C7831
6	6	A6	A6	A5	A5	A605	A605	A3605	A3605
7	___?	A7	A__?	A6	A6	A606	A606	A3606	A3606
8	8	B1	B1	B1	B1	B451	B451	B5451	B5451
9	9	B2	B2	B2	B2	B452	___?	B5452	B5452
10	10	A8	A8	C2	C2	C832	C832	C7832	C7832
11	11	A9	A9	A7	A7	A607	A607	A3607	A3607
12	12	B3	B3	A8	A8	A608	A608	A3608	A3608
13	13	B4	B__?	C3	C3	C833	C833	C7833	C7833
14	14	B5	B5	C4	C__?	C834	___?	C7834	___?
15	15	B6	B6	C5	C5	C835	C835	C7835	C7835
16	16	A10	A10	A9	A9	A609	A609	A3609	A3609
17	17	A11	A11	A10	A10	A610	A610	A3610	A3610
18	18	A12	A12	C6	C6	C836	C836	C7836	C7836
19	19	A13	A13	B3	B3	B453	B453	B5453	B5453
20	___?	B7	B7	B4	B4	B454	B454	B5454	B5454
21	21	A14	A14	B5	B__?	B455	B455	B5455	___?
22	22	A15	A15	B6	B6	B456	B456	B5456	B5456
23	23	B8	B8	B7	B7	B457	B457	B5457	B5457
24	24	A16	A16	B8	B8	B458	___?	B5458	B5458
25	25	A17	A__?	C7	C7	C837	C837	C7837	C7837
26	___?	A18	A18	C8	C8	C838	C838	C7838	C7838
27	27	A19	A19	C9	C9	C839	C839	C7839	___?
28	28	B9	B9	C10	C10	C840	C840	C7840	C7840
29	29	B10	B10	A11	A__?	A611	A611	A3611	A3611
30	30	B11	B11	A12	A12	A612	A612	A3612	A3612

53

CLERICAL ASSISTANT

Assume that each number and each set of numbers/letters listed (Example: 4, B6, C10, B5457, etc.) is an individual case.

In column A1, cases listed are from 1 through 30. These case numbers may be the case numbers of the first 30 cases issued by the court during a certain year, or they might represent the first 30 jury cases that were sent to trial, etc. Regardless of what the numbers represent, they are listed in a LOGICAL AND CONSISTENT order. In column A1 the order is very apparent. The cases are listed in SEQUENTIAL ORDER. That is: 1...2...3...4...5...6...etc. Therefore, in column A2, the case number which should come after case number 6 is case number 7. Easy enough. The case number which should come after case number 19 is case number 20. And the case number which should come after case number 25 is case number 26.

Column B1 also lists cases in sequential order. However, in this column there are 2 types of cases that are listed: "A TYPE" cases and "B TYPE" cases. Although the "Type A" and "Type B" cases are interspersed in the column, BOTH TYPES OF CASES ARE LISTED IN SEQUENTIAL ORDER. That is: A1, A2, A3, A4, A5, A6, A7, A8, A9...etc., and
B1, B2, B3, B4, B5, B6, B7, B8, B9...etc.

The case listed after case A6 therefore is case A7.
The case listed after case B3 therefore is case B4.
The case listed after case A16 therefore is case A17.

In column C1 there are 3 types of cases listed: "A CASES", "B CASES" and "C CASES".
The case between A2 and A4 is therefore case A3.
The case between C3 and C5 is therefore case C4.
The case between B4 and B6 is therefore case B5.
The case between C10 and A12 is therefore case A11.

(See the next page for the competed table.)

CLERICAL ASSISTANT

A1	A2	B1	B2	C1	C2	D1	D2	E1	E2
1	1	A1	A1	A1	A1	A601	A601	A3601	A3601
2	2	A2	A2	A2	A2	A602	A602	A3602	A3602
3	3	A3	A3	A3	A_3_?	A603	A603	A3603	A3603
4	4	A4	A4	A4	A4	A604	A604?	A3604	A3604
5	5	A5	A5	C1	C1	C831	C831	C7831	C7831
6	6	A6	A6	A5	A5	A605	A605	A3605	A3605
7	_7_?	A7	A_7_?	A6	A6	A606	A606	A3606	A3606
8	8	B1	B1	B1	B1	B451	B451	B5451	B5451
9	9	B2	B2	B2	B2	B452	B452?	B5452	B5452
10	10	A8	A8	C2	C2	C832	C832	C7832	C7832
11	11	A9	A9	A7	A7	A607	A607	A3607	A3607
12	12	B3	B3	A8	A8	A608	A608	A3608	A3608
13	13	B4	B_4_?	C3	C3	C833	C833	C7833	C7833
14	14	B5	B5	C4	C_4_?	C834	C834?	C7834	C7834
15	15	B6	B6	C5	C5	C835	C835	C7835	C7835
16	16	A10	A10	A9	A9	A609	A609	A3609	A3609
17	17	A11	A11	A10	A10	A610	A610	A3610	A3610
18	18	A12	A12	C6	C6	C836	C836	C7836	C7836
19	19	A13	A13	B3	B3	B453	B453	B5453	B5453
20	_20_?	B7	B7	B4	B4	B454	B454	B5454	B5454
21	21	A14	A14	B5	B_5_?	B455	B455	B5455	B5455
22	22	A15	A15	B6	B6	B456	B456	B5456	B5456
23	23	B8	B8	B7	B7	B457	B457	B5457	B5457
24	24	A16	A16	B8	B8	B458	B458?	B5458	B5458
25	25	A17	A_17_?	C7	C7	C837	C837	C7837	C7837
26	_26_?	A18	A18	C8	C8	C838	C838	C7838	C7838
27	27	A19	A19	C9	C9	C839	C839	C7839	C7839
28	28	B9	B9	C10	C10	C840	C840	C7840	C7840
29	29	B10	B10	A11	A_11_?	A611	A611	A3611	A3611
30	30	B11	B11	A12	A12	A612	A612	A3612	A3612

CLERICAL ASSISTANT

NUMBERS MANIPULATION EXERCISE (Fill in empty boxes)

	MON.	TUES.	WED.	THURS.	FRI.	Total Cases
Judge Baker	6		5	9	4	31
Judge Jones	5	4	7	5	9	30
Judge Chin	7	5	4	8	6	32
Judge Romero	8	6		6	7	32
Judge Novak	8	6	9	4	5	
Total Cases	34	28	30		31	

(Answers are on the following page.)

NEXT LOGICAL CASE EXERCISE (What are the answers to (1) (2) (3) (4) and (5)?

LOG OF CASES (MONDAY, OCTOBER 15, 2014) FOR JUDGES DALTON AND KEARNS			
Judge	Case Number	Civil/Criminal	Part
J. Dalton	C7638/01	Civil	6
J. Dalton	C7493/01	Civil	6
J. Kearns	D37867/01	Criminal	22
J. Kearns	D28658/01	Criminal	22
J. Dalton	(1)??	Civil	6
J. Kearns	D46294/01	(2)??	22
J. Dalton	C38876/01	(3)??	6
J. (4)??	C87635/01	Civil	6
J. (5)??	D76942/01	Criminal	22

Which of the following is the most logical choice for the number indicated? (Answers are on the next page)

(1) A. D87493/01   B. D28659/01   C. C67386/01   D. E28593/01

(2) A. Civil   B. Family   C. Supreme   D. Criminal

(3) A. Civil   B. Family   C. Supreme   D. Criminal

(4) A. Dalton   B. Kearns   C. Dalton or Kearns   D. None of the above

(5) A. Dalton   B. Kearns   C. Dalton or Kearns   D. None of the above

(Answers are on the following page.)

56

CLERICAL ASSISTANT

ANSWERS TO NUMBERS MANIPULATION EXERCISE (Filled-in bold)

	MON.	TUES.	WED.	THURS.	FRI.	Total Cases
Judge Baker	6	**7**	5	9	4	31
Judge Jones	5	4	7	5	9	**30**
Judge Chin	7	5	4	8	6	30
Judge Romero	8	6	**5**	6	7	32
Judge Novak	8	6	9	4	5	32
Total Cases	34	28	30	**32**	31	**155**

ANSWERS TO NEXT LOGICAL CASE EXERCISE- What are answers to (1) (2) (3) (4) (5)?

LOG OF CASES (MONDAY, OCTOBER 15, 2014) FOR JUDGES DALTON AND KEARNS			
Judge	Case Number	Civil/Criminal	Part
J. Dalton	C7638/10	Civil	6
J. Dalton	C7493/10	Civil	6
J. Kearns	D37867/10	Criminal	22
J. Kearns	D28658/10	Criminal	22
J. Dalton	(1)??	Civil	6
J. Kearns	D46294/10	(2)??	22
J. Dalton	C38876/10	(3)??	6
J. (4)??	C87635/10	Civil	6
J. (5)??	D76942/10	Criminal	22

Which of the following is the most logical choice for the number indicated in bold? **(Answers are in bold and underlined.)**

(1) A. D87493/10   B. D28659/10   **C. C67386/10**   D. E28593/10

(2) A. Civil   B. Family   C. Supreme   **D. Criminal**

(3) **A. Civil**   B. Family   C. Supreme   D. Criminal

(4) **A. Dalton**   B. Kearns   C. Dalton or Kearns   D. None of the above

(5) A. Dalton   **B. Kearns**   C. Dalton or Kearns   D. None of the above

CLERICAL ASSISTANT

Example 1: Record keeping

DAILY LIST OF TRIALS				
Judge	Case Type (Civil/Criminal)	Case Number	Money Award (Civil)	Conviction (Criminal)
J. Binkins	Civil	C9642/09	X	
J. Rodriguez	Civil	C8682/09	16,000	
J. Binkins	Criminal	D82943/11		YES
J. Welmor	Civil	C4325/09	32,000	
J. Binkins	Criminal	D7829/11		YES
J. Rodriguez	Civil	C8793/11	65,000	
J. Fondaro	Civil	C2263/09	29,500	
J. Binkins	Civil	C3729/09	X	
J. Chu	Criminal	D86739/11		YES
J. Novatov	Criminal	???		NO
J. Rodriguez	Civil	C7354/08	X	
J. Harkins	Civil	C4658/07	42,500	

Using the above table, complete the summary table below and answer the 4 questions on the following page.

SUMMARY OF DAILY LIST OF TRIALS				
Judge	Number of Cases (Civil)	Number of Cases (Criminal)	Number of Cases With A Money Award	Number of Cases With A Conviction
J. Binkins				
J. Rodriguez				
J. Welmor				
J. Fondaro				
J. Chu				
J. Novatov				
J. Harkins				
Total Cases				

CLERICAL ASSISTANT

1. Which Judge tried the most civil cases?

    A. Binkins   B. Harkins   C. Welmor   D. Rodriguez

2. A possible case number for the missing case number "???" tried by Judge Novatov is:

    A. C1893/09   B. D3819/11   C. C4326/09   D. C86740/11

3. For how many civil cases was there a money award?

    A. 3   B. 4   C. 5   D. 2

4. The maximum money award was in a trial before Judge:

    A. Rodriguez   B. Fondaro   C. Welmor   D. Harkins

COMPLETED SUMMARY TABLE

SUMMARY OF DAILY LIST OF TRIALS

Judge	Number of Cases (Civil)	Number of Cases (Criminal)	Number of Cases With A Money Award	Number of Cases With A Conviction
J. Binkins	2 //	2 //		2
J. Rodriguez	3 ///		2 //	
J. Welmor	1 /		1 /	
J. Fondaro	1 /		1 /	
J. Chu		1 /		1
J. Novatov		1 /		
J. Harkins	1 /		1 /	
Total Cases	8	4	5	3

(See next page for answers 1 – 4.)

CLERICAL ASSISTANT

Answers to the 4 questions on the preceding page:

1. D Rodriguez
He tried a total of 3 civil cases.

2. B D3819/11
The case was a criminal case and all criminal case file numbers begin with a "D". The only choice that begins with a "D" is choice "B."

3. C 5
This is the intersection of the "Total Cases" row and the "Number of Cases With A Money Award" column.

4. A Rodriguez ($65,000)

TABLE TEST-TAKING SUGGESTIONS

1. Briefly look at the main table and the supplementary tables (if they are provided) to see how the information will be displayed. Become familiar with the structure of the tables and how they relate to each other.

2. By using the information in the main table, fill out the supplementary tables. (Sometimes the supplementary tables may be provided. Other times you may have to create a table to suit your needs.)

3. Concentrate while posting from the main table to the supplementary tables to avoid mistakes.

4. As you post the information from the main table to the supplementary tables, maintain your finger on the main table line of information that you are posting to the supplementary tables. If you need to, use marks next to the information that you have just posted (/ , X , + , etc.).

5. Concentrate on speed and accuracy. Make sure that all your postings are correct the first time so that you will not lose precious time trying to figure out where you went wrong.

6. Make sure that your totals in the supplementary tables are equal and that the total number of items in the supplementary table equals the total number of items in the main table.

7. Use the filled-out tables to answer the questions. Some questions may be answered directly by skimming the information in the main table. However, some questions require the use of one of the filled-out supplementary tables (especially when the main table contains 25 or more lines of information). If there is any way for you to double-check your answer, quickly do so.

8. If you finish the test, keep checking your answers until the allotted time for the test has expired.

CLERICAL ASSISTANT

Example 2: Record keeping (Simple Example)

Using the information in the 3 tables on this page, fill-in the 3 summary tables on the next page and then answer the 5 questions.

LOG OF CASES (October 1, 2011: Monday)			
Part	Date Filed	Case Status	Money Award
Part 2	6/17/06	Settled	$12,500
Part 6	5/21/07	Dismissed	None
Part 7	8/14/08	Defaulted	None
Part 8	4/21/06	Settled	$17,500
Part 12	9/15/07	Adjourned	None
Part 12	11/07/09	Settled	$19,000

LOG OF CASES (October 2, 2011: Tuesday)			
Part 2	3/17/08	Adjourned	None
Part 2	5/24/08	Settled	$17,000
Part 6	12/7/07	Dismissed	None
Part 7	7/26/08	Defaulted	None
Part 8	4/21/08	Adjourned	None
Part 12	4/26/09	Settled	$21,500

LOG OF CASES (October 3, 2011: Wednesday)			
Part	Date Filed	Case Status	Money Award
Part 2	3/11/06	Settled	None
Part 6	2/9/07	Dismissed	None
Part 7	5/16/08	Settled	$12,000
Part 8	9/22/06	Settled	$7,500
Part 12	4/01/07	Adjourned	None
Part 12	4/13/09	Adjourned	None

CLERICAL ASSISTANT

SUMMARY OF CASES (BY CASE STATUS)
October 1, 2011 - October 3, 2011

Case Activity	10/1/11	10/2/11	10/3/11	Total Cases
Adjourned				
Defaulted				
Dismissed				
Settled - with money award				
Settled - with no money award				
Total # of Cases				

SUMMARY OF CASES (BY YEAR FILED)
October 1, 2011 - October 3, 2011

Year Filed	10/1/01	10/2/01	10/3/01	Total Cases
1996				
1997				
1998				
1999				
Total # of Cases				

SUMMARY OF CASES (BY PART)
October 1, 2011 - October 3, 2011

Part	Adjourned	Dismissed	Defaulted	Settled - with no money award	Settled - with money award	Total Cases
Part 2						
Part 6						
Part 7						
Part 8						
Part12						
Total						

CLERICAL ASSISTANT

Answer the following 5 questions based on the information in the preceding tables.

1. How many cases were filed during 2007?

    A. 2   B. 4   C. 5   D. 3

2. How many cases were settled on Tuesday with a money award?

    A. 1   B. 2   C. 3   D. 4

3. What was the total number of cases adjourned or defaulted on 10/1/11?

    A. 1   B. 2   C. 3   D. 4

4. What was the total number of cases dismissed for the three days?

    A. 3   B. 2   C. 1   D. 0

5. What is the total number of cases adjourned in Part 2 and Part 12?

    A. 1   B. 2   C. 3   D. 4

CLERICAL ASSISTANT

Filled-In Tables for Example 2

SUMMARY OF CASES (BY CASE STATUS)
October 1, 2011 - October 3, 2011

Case Activity	10/1/11	10/2/11	10/3/11	Total Cases
Adjourned	1 /	2 //	2 //	5
Defaulted	1 /	1 /	--	2
Dismissed	1 /	1 /	1 /	3
Settled - with money award	3 ///	2 //	2 //	7
Settled - with no money award	--	--	1 /	1
Total # of Cases	6	6	6	18

SUMMARY OF CASES (BY YEAR FILED)
October 1, 2011 - October 3, 2011

Year Filed	10/1/11	10/2/11	10/3/11	Total Cases
2006	2 //	--	2 //	4
2007	2 //	1 /	2 //	5
2008	1 /	4 ////	1 /	6
2009	1 /	1 /	1 /	3
Total # of Cases	6	6	6	18

SUMMARY OF CASES (BY PART)
October 1, 2011 - October 3, 2011

Part	Adjourned	Dismissed	Defaulted	Settled - with no money award	Settled - with money award	Total Cases
Part 2	1 /	--	--	1 /	2 //	4
Part 6	--	3 ///	--	--	--	3
Part 7	--	--	2 //	--	1 /	3
Part 8	1 /	--	--	--	2 //	3
Part 12	3 ///	--	--	--	2 //	5
Total	5	3	2	1	7	18

CLERICAL ASSISTANT

Answers For Example 2 Questions

1. How many cases were filed during 2007?

    Answer: C. 5

To get this answer you could look in the "Date Filed" column in the "LOG OF CASES", for October1, 2011, October 2, 2011 and October 3, 2011 tables and count those cases that were filed in 2007. The year that a case is filed is the last two digits of the date. Example: 11/16/07. You can also get the same answer by looking in the table of "SUMMARY OF CASES (BY YEAR FILED) October 1, 2011 - October 3, 2011," specifically at the intersection of "Total Cases" and "2007" columns.

2. How many cases were settled on Tuesday with a money award?

    Answer: B. 2

By using the "LOG OF CASES" for Tuesday, 10/02/11, count the cases that were settled with a money award. You can get the same answer from the table "SUMMARY OF CASES (BY CASE STATUS) October 1, 2011 - October 3, 2011" and using the number at the intersection of the columns "10/2/11" and "Settled - with money award" columns.

3. How many cases were adjourned or defaulted on Monday?

    Answer: B. 2

Total the October 1, 2011 adjourned and the October 1, 2011 defaulted cases listed in the "LOG OF CASES" for October 1, 2011, or add the number of 10/01/11 defaulted and the number of 10/01/11 adjourned cases from the table "SUMMARY OF CASES (BY CASE STATUS) October 1, 2011 - October 3, 2011" for 10/01/11.

4. What was the total number of cases dismissed for the three days?

    Answer: A. 3

Total the cases dismissed "LOG OF CASES," for October 1, 2011, October 2, 2011 and October 3, 2011, or get the same total by using the "SUMMARY OF CASES (BY CASE STATUS) October 1, 2011 - October 3, 2011", table.

5. What is the total number of cases adjourned in Part 2 and Part 12?

    Answer: D. 4

Use either the table "LOG OF CASES, October 1, 2011 - October 3, 2011," or the table "SUMMARY OF CASES (BY PART) October 1, 2011 - October 3, 2011.

CLERICAL ASSISTANT

Example 3: Using the information in this table, fill in the tables on the next page and then answer the 15 subsequent questions.

LOG OF CASES Monday - Friday				
Judge	Date Filed	Day Appeared On Court Calendar	Case Status	Money Award
Nordstrom	2/16/07	Monday	Adjourned	-----
Washington	8/9/06	Monday	Settled	X
Nordstrom	11/16/08	Monday	Defaulted	-----
Sanchez	4/22/07	Monday	Dismissed	-----
Fong	9/22/06	Monday	Adjourned	-----
Bratton	1/13/07	Monday	Dismissed	-----
Johnson	5/24/06	Tuesday	Settled	$64,000
Fuller	6/7/08	Tuesday	Settled	$22,000
Nordstrom	12/25/07	Tuesday	Defaulted	-----
Sanchez	2/21/06	Tuesday	Settled	X
Johnson	5/26/04	Tuesday	Settled	$31,500
Bratton	8/16/06	Wednesday	Dismissed	-----
Fong	5/12/07	Wednesday	Settled	$11,000
Bratton	3/16/08	Wednesday	Defaulted	-----
Bratton	2/22/06	Wednesday	Adjourned	-----
Nordstrom	7/11/07	Thursday	Settled	X
Johnson	8/17/08	Thursday	Adjourned	-----
Sanchez	3/24/08	Thursday	Settled	$43,000
Fong	9/16/07	Friday	Dismissed	-----
Bratton	4/26/08	Friday	Defaulted	-----
Sanchez	5/21/08	Friday	Adjourned	-----
Nordstrom	8/25/05	Friday	Settled	$41,500
Fong	6/17/08	Friday	Settled	$25,600

CLERICAL ASSISTANT

SUMMARY OF CASES (BY CASE STATUS): Monday - Friday							
Status	Monday	Tuesday	Wednesday	Thursday	Friday	Total Cases
Adjourned						
Defaulted						
Dismissed						
Settled - with money award						
Settled - with no money award						
Total Cases On Calendar						
Year Filed						
2004						
2005						
2006						
2007						
2008						
Total Cases On Calendar						

SUMMARY OF CASES (BY JUDGE): Monday - Friday						
Judge	Adjourned	Dismissed	Defaulted	Settled - with no money award	Settled - with money award	Total Cases
Nordstrom						
Washington						
Sanchez						
Fong						
Bratton						
Johnson						
Fuller						
Total						

CLERICAL ASSISTANT

Answer the following 15 questions based on the information in the preceding tables.

1. How many cases were filed during 2007?
   A. 4   B. 5   C. 6   D. 7

2. How many cases were settled on Monday, Tuesday and Wednesday with a money award?
   A. 4   B. 5   C. 6   D. 7

3. What is the total number of cases adjourned or defaulted on Wednesday?
   A. 1   B. 2   C. 3   D. 4

4. How many cases were settled on Monday and Tuesday with no money award?
   A. 3   B. 2   C. 1   D. 0

5. What is the total number of cases adjourned by Judge Nordstrom and Bratton?
   A. 1   B. 2   C. 3   D. 4

6. Which Judge has the greatest number of "dismissed" cases?
   A.   Bratton
   B.   Fong
   C.   Sanchez
   D.   Nordstrom

7. Of the following pairs of 2 Judges, which 2 Judges have the same number of cases "Settled - with no money award" as "Settled - with money award?"
   A. Fuller and Johnson
   B. Nordstrom and Sanchez
   C. Fong and Washington
   D. Sanchez and Fong

8. What is the total number of cases "Settled - with no money award" and "Settled - with money award"?
   A. 8   B. 9   C. 10   D. 11

CLERICAL ASSISTANT

9. A total of 6 of the cases were filed in which of the following years?

    A. 2008   B. 2007   C. 2006   D. 2005

10. Which two Judges did not adjourn any cases?

    A. Johnson and Fuller

    B. Fong and Washington

    C. Fuller and Sanchez

    D. Washington and Fuller

11. The total of cases "Settled - with money award" exceeded the total of cases "Settled - with no money award" by:

    A. 3   B. 4   C. 5   D. 6

12. The total number of cases Dismissed and Defaulted exceeded the total number of cases adjourned by:

    A. 3   B. 4   C. 5   D. 6

13. Cases filed in either 2004 or 2005 appeared on the calendar on which days?

    A. Monday and Tuesday

    B. Tuesday and Wednesday

    C. Thursday and Friday

    D. Tuesday and Friday

14. What is the total number of cases filed in 2006 and 2007?

    A. 13   C. 15

    B. 14   D. 12

15. The two judges who heard the least number of cases were:

    A. Nordstrom and Johnson

    B. Johnson and Fuller

    C. Fuller and Washington

    D. Sanchez and Washington

The filled-in tables are on the next page, followed by answers (1-15).

CLERICAL ASSISTANT

SUMMARY OF CASES (BY CASE STATUS): Monday - Friday

Status	Monday	Tuesday	Wed.	Thursday	Friday	Total Cases
Adjourned	2 //		1 /	1 /	1 /	5
Defaulted	1 /	1 /	1 /		1 /	4
Dismissed	2 //		1 /		1 /	4
Settled - with money award		3 ///	1 /	1 /	2 //	7
Settled - with no money award	1 /	1 /		1 /		3
Total Cases On Calendar	6	5	4	3	5	23
Year Filed						
2004		1 /				1
2005					1 /	1
2006	2 //	2 //	2 //			6
2007	3 ///	1 /	1 /	1 /	1 /	7
2008	1 /	1 /	1 /	2 //	3 ///	8
Total Cases On Calendar	6	5	4	3	5	23

SUMMARY OF CASES (BY JUDGE): Monday - Friday

Judge	Adjourned	Dismissed	Defaulted	Settled - with no money award	Settled - with money award	Total Cases
Nordstrom	1 /		2 //	1 /	1 /	5
Washington				1 /		1
Sanchez	1 /	1 /		1 /	1 /	4
Fong	1 /	1 /			2 //	4
Bratton	1 /	2 //	2 //			5
Johnson	1 /				2 //	3
Fuller					1 /	1
Total	5	4	4	3	7	23

(Answers for questions 1-15 are on the following page.)

CLERICAL ASSISTANT

1. How many cases were filed during 2007?
Answer: D. 7
(To get this answer you could look in the "Date Filed" column in the "LOG OF CASES, Monday - Friday" table and count those cases that were filed in 2007. The year that a case is filed is the last two digits of the date. Example: 10/15/07. You can also get the same answer by looking in the table of "SUMMARY OF CASES (BY CASE STATUS) Monday - Friday", specifically in the "Total Cases" column for 2007.)

2. How many cases were settled on Monday, Tuesday and Wednesday with a money award?
Answer: A. 4
(By using "LOG OF CASES, Monday - Friday," count the Monday, Tuesday and Wed. cases that were settled with a money award. You can get the same answer from the table "SUMMARY OF CASES (BY CASE STATUS)" by totaling the intersections of the Monday, Tuesday and Wednesday columns and "Settled - with money award" row.)

3. What is the total number of cases adjourned or defaulted on Wednesday?
Answer: B. 2
(Total the Wed. adjourned and the Wed. defaulted cases listed in the "LOG OF CASES, Monday - Friday" or add the number of Wednesday defaulted and the number of Wednesday Adjourned cases from the table "SUMMARY OF CASES (BY CASE STATUS) Monday - Friday.")

4. How many cases were settled on Tuesday and Thursday with no money award?
Answer: B. 2
(Total the cases settled with no money award in the "LOG OF CASES, Monday - Friday" or get the same total by using either the "SUMMARY OF CASES (BY CASE STATUS) Monday - Friday" or "SUMMARY OF CASES (BY PART) Monday - Friday.")

5. What is the total number of cases adjourned by Judge Nordstrom and Judge Bratton?
Answer: B. 2
(Use either the table "LOG OF CASES Monday - Friday," or the table "SUMMARY OF CASES (BY JUDGE) Monday - Friday.)

6. Which Judge has the greatest number of "dismissed" cases?
Answer: A. Bratton
(Use either the table "SUMMARY OF CASES (BY JUDGE) Monday-Friday" or the provided "LOG OF CASES Monday-Friday.")

7. Of the following pairs of 2 Judges, which 2 Judges have the same number of cases "Settled - with no money award" as "Settled - with money award?"
Answer: B. Nordstrom and Sanchez
(Use "SUMMARY OF CASES (BY JUDGE).)

8. What is total # of cases "Settled-with no money award" and "Settled-with money award"?
Answer: C. 10
(Use "SUMMARY OF CASES (BY CASE STATUS) Monday-Friday" table or "LOG OF CASES Monday-Friday," or "Summary of Cases (By Judge)."

CLERICAL ASSISTANT

9. A total of 6 of the cases were filed in which of the following years?
Answer: C. 2006
(Use "SUMMARY OF CASES (BY YEAR FILED) Monday-Friday" table or "LOG OF CASES Monday-Friday.")

10. Which two Judges did not adjourn any cases?
Answer: D. Washington and Fuller
(Use "SUMMARY OF CASES (BY JUDGE) Monday-Friday" table or "LOG OF CASES Monday-Friday.")

11. The total of cases "Settled - with money award" exceeded the total of cases "Settled - with no money award" by:
Answer: B. 4
(Use "SUMMARY OF CASES (BY CASE STATUS) Monday-Friday", or "SUMMARY OF CASES (BY JUDGE) Monday-Friday" or "LOG OF CASES Monday-Friday.")

12. Total number of cases Dismissed and Defaulted exceeded total number of cases adjourned by:
Answer: A. 3
(Use "SUMMARY OF CASES (BY CASE STATUS) Monday-Friday", or "SUMMARY OF CASES (BY JUDGE) Monday-Friday" or "LOG OF CASES Monday-Friday.")

13. Cases filed in either 2004 or 2005 appeared on the calendar on which days?
Answer: D. Tuesday and Friday
(Use "SUMMARY OF CASES (BY YEAR FILED) Monday-Friday" table or "LOG OF CASES Monday-Friday.")

14. What is the total number of cases filed in 2006 and 2007?
Answer: A. 13
(Use "SUMMARY OF CASES (BY YEAR FILED) Monday-Friday" table or "LOG OF CASES Monday-Friday.")

15. The two judges who heard the least number of cases were:
Answer: C. Fuller and Washington
(Use "SUMMARY OF CASES (BY JUDGE) Monday-Friday" table or "LOG OF CASES Monday-Friday.")

CLERICAL ASSISTANT

READING, UNDERSTANDING AND INTERPRETING WRITTEN MATERIAL 5

(Reading Comprehension)

These questions assess candidates' ability to understand brief written passages.

Candidates will be provided with short written passages from which words or phrases have been removed.

Candidates will be required to select from four alternatives the word or phrase that logically completes the sentence within the passage when inserted for the missing word or phrase.*

CLERICAL ASSISTANT

Example 1:

The dispute in question was __1__ Jamed Odell and Susan Watkins, who stated that she was suing on __2__. The case was tried last Wednesday, at which time the __3__ rendered a verdict in favor of the plaintiff. The defendant immediately __4__ a Notice of Appeal. Two days __5__ the plaintiff and defendant settled the case and the defendant discontinued the appeal.

1. A. among   B. amongs   C. between   D. beyond
2. A. principal   B. princepal   C. princeple   D. principle
3. A. jury   B. witness   C. lawyer   D. teacher
4. A. denied   B. filed   C. claimed   D. disregarded
5. A. before   B. preceeding   C. precedent   D. later

Answers for Example 1:

1. C) *between* is used when referring to 2 persons; *among* when referring to 3 or more persons
2. D) *principle* (a concept or one's conviction) as opposed to the *principal* of a school.
3. A) *jury* is the only group among the choices that can render a verdict (general knowledge)
4. B) *filed* a court paper - the Notice of Appeal.
5. D) *later* because the settlement occurred <u>after</u> the filing of the Notice of Appeal.

Example 2:

Following a ____(1)____, community members may be on their own for a period of time because of the size of the area affected, lost communications, and impassable roads. The Community Emergency Response Team (CERT) program supports local response capability by training volunteers to organize themselves and spontaneous volunteers at the disaster site, to provide immediate assistance to victims, and to collect disaster intelligence to support responders' efforts when they arrive. In the classroom, participants learn about the hazards they face and ways to prepare for them. CERT members are ____(2)____ basic organizational skills that they can use to help themselves, their loved ones, and their neighbors until help arrives.

1. A. weekends   B. holidays   C. parades   D. disaster
2. A. indoctrinated   B. explained   C. taught   D. accustomed

CLERICAL ASSISTANT

Answers for Example 2:
1. D) the subject of the entire paragraph is *disasters* (in this case singular "**a** *disaster*")
2. C) students are *taught* in classrooms

Answers for the following questions (3 - 8) are on page 78.

Example 3:

Although every Court Officer is a peace officer and is authorized to carry __1__ gun, the primary tool that a Court Officer uses is __2__ mind. __3__ have been very few occasions when a Court Officer has been __4__ to take a __5__ out of her holster, and fewer still when she has had the need to discharge it.

1. A) two   B) concealed   C) deadly   D) a
2. A) their   B) there   C) her   D) them
3. A) their   B) there   C) their's   D) there's
4. A) need   B) required   C) thinking   D) necessitated
5. A) knives   B) knife   C) gun   D) blade

Example 4:

__1__ non-uniformed court employees, Court Officers must spend some time each morning getting into uniform. Because they are required to be in uniform at the start of their __2__ of duty, the Office of Court Administration __3__ Court Officers for such time by giving them an extra __4__ week of leave each year. This additional week brings up to five weeks the total annual leave __5__ to which Court Officers are entitled their first year on the job.

1. A) like   B) unlike   C) as   D) same
2. A) end   B) start   C) tour   D) responsibility
3. A) charges   B) compensates   C) forfeits   D) aleviates
4. A) three   B) four   C) one   D) two
5. A) hours   B) months   C) weeks   D) weekends

Example 5:

The __1__ car was stolen on Sunday. The plaintiff said that because of the theft, he was not able to __2__ his scheduled trial on Monday. He stated that the __3__ reason he was absent was that the train station is five miles from his home. The Judge did not __4__ and therefore dismissed __5__ case.

CLERICAL ASSISTANT

1. A) defendants   B) plaintiffs   C) defendent's   D) plaintiff's
2. A) walk   B) attend   C) talk   D) hike
3. A) principle   B) principel   C) principal   D) princeple
4. A) talk   B) agree   C) see   D) hear
5. A) their   B) your   C) her   D) his

Example 6:

___(1)___ are one of the most common hazards in the United States. Flood effects can be local, impacting a ___(2)___ or community, or very large, affecting entire river basins and multiple states. However, all floods are ___(3)___ alike. Some floods develop slowly, sometimes over a period of days. But flash floods can develop quickly, sometimes in just a few ___(3)___ and without any visible signs of rain. Flash floods often have a dangerous wall of roaring water that carries rocks, mud, and other debris and can sweep away most things in its path. Overland flooding occurs outside a defined river or stream, such as when a levee is breached, but still can be destructive. Flooding can also occur when a dam breaks, producing effects similar to flash floods. Be aware of flood hazards no matter where you live, but especially if you live in a ___(5)___ area, near water or downstream from a dam. Even very small streams, gullies, creeks, culverts, dry stream beds, or low-lying ground that appear harmless in dry weather can flood. Every state is at risk from this hazard.

1. A. Emergencies   B. Fires   C. Parades   D. Floods
2. A. countries   B. nations   C. neighborhood   D. continents
3. A. very   B. extremely   C. strangely   D. not
4. A. months   B. minutes   C. decades   D. years
5. A. low-lying   B. high-altitude C. high-crime   D. well-lit

Example 7:

Mondays and the day after a holiday are usually ___(1)___ volume days for most courts. To prepare for the increased activity, additional Court Officers are assigned to security and information posts. The heaviest volume of persons occurs ___(2)___ the hours of 9:30 AM and 11:30 AM.

1. A) low   B) moderate   C) high   D) decreased
2. A) subsequent   B) among   C) after   D) between

CLERICAL ASSISTANT

Example 8:

Technological hazards __(1)__ hazardous materials incidents and nuclear power plant failures. Usually, little or no warning precedes incidents involving technological hazards. In many cases, victims may not know they have been affected until many years later. For example, health problems caused by hidden toxic waste sites—like that at Love Canal, near Niagara Falls, New York—surfaced years after initial exposure. The number of technological incidents is __(2)__, mainly as a result of the increased number of new substances and the opportunities for human error inherent in the use of these materials.

1. A. exclude   B. preclude   C. precede   D. include
2. A. decreasing   B. diminishing   C. escalating   D. static

Example 9:

An employee __(1)__ develops an unacceptable punctuality or attendance record shall be informally counseled and a counseling form shall be submitted to the Chief Clerk. The form shall not be __(2)__ in the employee's permanent file, but shall be kept separate as a reference for eighteen months.

1. A) which   B) whom   C) whose   D) who
2. A) discarded   B) pulled   C) filed   D) withdrawn

Example 10:

All Court Officers must attend periodic instruction in such subjects as CPR, bomb threats procedure and public service. To attend the classes, all Court Officers must travel __(1)__ 111 Centre Street, where the classes __(2)__ held.

1. A) two   B) too   C) to   D) from
2. A) is   B) were   C) was   D) are

CLERICAL ASSISTANT

Answers for Example 3:

1. D) *a* (*two* is plural, *concealed* and *deadly* not grammatically correct)
2. C) *her* (singular adjective for singular *mind*)
3. B) *their* and *their's* are possessive; *there's* means *there is*
4. B) *required* (other choices not logical in terms of meaning)
5. C) *gun* (topic of paragraph is *guns* and not *knives*)

Answers for Example 4:

1. B) *unlike* - because paragraphs deals with different requirements of Court Officers
2. C) *tour* is the only choice which makes any sense
3. B) *compensates* is the only choice which indicates rewarding officers
4. C) *one* (singular adjective for singular *week*)
5. C) *weeks* of leave - the subject of the paragraph

Answers for Example 5:

1. D) *plaintiff's* (singular possessive)
2. B) *attend* (only grammatically correct choice)
3. C) *principal* (correct spelling and correct word - *not* principle)
4. B) *agree* (logic, because Judge *dismissed* his case)
5. D) *his* (singular and masculine - to agree with subject at beginning of paragraph)

Answers for Example 6:

1. D) The subject <u>floods</u> continues in the next sentence.
2. C) *Neighborhood is singular*, others are plural.
3. D) Sentence speaks about *differences* in floods.
4. B) The *opposite* of slowly (minutes).
5. A) Risk of floods is to *low-lying* areas.

Answers for Example 7:

1. C) *high* (to agree with *increased activity*)
2. D) *between* (between the 2 times)

CLERICAL ASSISTANT

Answer for Example 8:

1. D) include   Hazardous material incidents and nuclear power plant failures are two *examples* of technological hazards.
2. C) escalating (as a result of *increased* number ....)

Answers for Example 9:

1. D) *who* (referring to a person and not possessive)
2. C) *filed* (logic)

Answers for Example 10:

1. C) *to* (instead of *from*, and not *two* (2) or *too* (extreme))
2. D) *are* (plural and present tense)

CLERICAL ASSISTANT

NUMBER FACILITY   6

These questions assess candidates' ability to perform basic calculations involving addition, subtraction, multiplication, division and percentages.

These questions do not require use of a calculator and calculators <u>will not</u> be permitted at the test center.*

CLERICAL ASSISTANT

NUMBER FACILITY

These questions require candidates to perform basic calculations involving addition, subtraction, multiplication, division and percentages. Information is presented in numerical format using forms typically found in a court setting. These questions do not require use of a calculator and calculators will not be permitted at the test center.

Percentages review:

20 per cent   =   .20   =   20%

Examples:

1.) 80 is what percent of 200?

Procedure: Divide 80 by 200

Answer: 40 %, or .40

2.) 60 percent of 30 equals what number ?

Procedure: Multiply 30 by .60

Answer: 18

3.) 18 is 90 percent of what number ?

Procedure: Divide 18 by .90

Answer: 20

CLERICAL ASSISTANT

Number Facility Warm-Up

1. (Percentage and subtraction question) On Monday 120 new employees started working in the NYS Civil Court. Of those new employees, 20 per cent of them live in Brooklyn.

   The number of employees who live outside of Brooklyn is:

   A. 100   B. 94   C. 104   D. None of the above.

---

2. (Addition and subtraction question) In criminal court, Part A, there were 242 spectators. In Part B there were 325 spectators. In the entire criminal court there were a total of 827 spectators.

   How many spectators were there in all the parts, not including Parts A and B?

   A. 160   B. 260   C. 360   D. None of the above

---

3. (Percentage and subtraction question) In the file room there are 800 files. Your supervisor tells you to take out 30 per cent of the files and put them in the next room.

   How many files should you put into the next room?

   A. 420   B. 240   C. 280   D. None of the above.

---

4. (Division question) In the file room there are 2,624 files. Your job is to divide the files into four equal stacks so that each stack can be put into a separate room.

   How many files must each stack contain?

   A. 665   B. 656   C. 566   D. None of the above.

---

5. (Percentage question) Select the choice which contains two equal amounts.

   A. .25 and 1/3   B. 33% and 1/4   C. .10 and 1/10   D. 22 per cent and 1/5

CLERICAL ASSISTANT

6. (Multiplication and subtraction question) A supervisor distributes 24 cases to each of his five employees. If the supervisor originally had 162 cases, how many cases remain undistributed?

A. 24 B. 42 C. 120 D. None of the above

7. (Addition, subtraction, division) A large court has 560 employees. On one day during the flu season, 10 per cent of the staff are absent due to sickness and another 5 per cent are out due to scheduled leave. Of those present during the day, 310 are assigned to the Civil Office and the rest of the employees are assigned to the Landlord and Tenant Office. How many employees are assigned to the Landlord and Tenant Office?

A) 310 B) 84 C) 250 D) 166

Answers: 1. D (Should be 96.) 2. B 3. B 4. B 5. C 6. B 7. D

If I had an hour to solve a problem I'd spend 55 minutes thinking about the problem and 5 minutes solving it. – *Albert Einstein*

Success is the sum of small efforts, repeated day in and day out. – *Robert Collier*

CLERICAL ASSISTANT

The following are questions involving forms "usually found in a court setting".

Number of Warrants To Be Processed

Date warrants received in the mail	Number of warrants received
Monday	110
Tuesday	85
Wednesday	105
Thursday	75
Friday	125
Total warrants to be processed	500

1. The supervisor of the warrant room supervises 10 Clerical Assistants. On Monday morning he is handed the above table of warrants to be processed. He examines the warrants and immediately rejects 50 warrants because they did not include the case number. If the supervisor wishes to divide the remaining warrants to be processed equally among his staff, how many warrants should he give to each employee?

A) 50

B) 40

C) 45

D) None of the above.

2. If the supervisor distributes only 80 per cent of the 450 warrants, how many warrants will not be distributed?

A) 400

B) 360

C) 90

D) None of the above.

3. At the end of the day, the supervisor has 100 warrants that he did not distribute and also 25 warrants not processed. What percentage of the 500 warrants have not been processed?

A) 15 per cent

B) 20 per cent

C) 25 per cent

D) None of the above.

4. The warrants received on one specific day of the week represents 25 per cent of the total warrants received during the week. That day is:

A) Monday

B) Tuesday

C) Wednesday

D) None of the above.

Answers: 1. C   2. C   3. C   4. D (Should be Friday, 125.)

CLERICAL ASSISTANT

The following are questions involving forms "usually found in a court setting".

The employees listed in the table below are assigned to the certifications unit. In a seven hour work-day the employees processed the following number of certifications:

Employee Name	Number of Certifications Processed
Helen Johnson	33
Fred Erikson	39
Bernice Vasquez	49
Mark Williams	43
Peter Fong	37
Eleanor Burke	39
Total Certifications Processed	240

Upon review by a supervisor, 60 certifications that were processed were found to be incorrectly filled out and were therefore voided.

1. What is the average number of certifications (excluding voided certifications) that were completed by each employee?

A. 30

B. 40

C. 43

D. None of the above.

2. What percentage of processed certifications were subsequently voided?

A. 20 %

B. 25 %

C. 30 %

D. 35 %

3. The two employees that together processed exactly 1/3 of the certifications are:

A. Eleanor Burke and Peter Fong

B. Mark Williams and Peter Fong

C. Mark Williams and Eleanor Burke

D. Helen Johnson and Peter Fong

4. If in order to reduce processing errors, the supervisor decides to distribute 30 certifications to be processed to each employee, how many employees would he need to distribute the 240 certifications?

A. 6

B. 4

C. 9

D. None of the above

Answers:

1. A
2. B
3. B
4. D (Answer is 8 employees... 3 X 8 = 240.)

CLERICAL ASSISTANT

The following are questions involving forms "usually found in a court setting".

The following table lists Judges and the cases they handled on Monday, June 21, 2015.

Judge	Case Number	Case Type	Disposed	Adjourned
J. Walker	3758/2005	Criminal	YES	
J. Eckert	4628/2006	Civil		YES
J. Williams	3199/2006	Criminal		YES
J. Rodriguez	3425/2005	Civil	YES	
J. Walinsky	3216/2006	Criminal	YES	
J. Chin	1324/2005	Criminal	YES	
J. Barnard	4421/2006	Civil		YES
J. Chaiken	6564/2006	Civil	YES	

1. The percentage of cases that were adjourned is:

A. 37.5 %

B. 30 %

C. 40 %

D. None of the above

2. The percentage of criminal cases that were adjourned is:

A. 25 %

B. 50 %

C. 70 %

D. None of the above

3. The percentage of civil cases that were disposed is:

A. 25 %

B. 50 %

C. 70 %

D. None of the above

4. Civil cases comprise what percentage of total cases?

A. 25 %

B. 50 %

C. 70 %

D. None of the above

Answers:

1. A   2. A   3. B   4. B

CLERICAL ASSISTANT

More Practice questions:

1. (Percentage and subtraction question) On Monday 240 new employees started working in the NYS Unified Court System. Of those new employees, 40 per cent of them live in NYC. The number of employees who live in New York City is:
   A. 100
   B. 94
   C. 96
   D. None of the above.

2. (Addition and subtraction question) In parts A, B and C in supreme court there are a total of 760 spectators. In Part A there are 255 spectators. In Part B there are 240 spectators. How many spectators are there in Part C?
   A. 265
   B. 260
   C. 365
   D. None of the above

3. (Percentage and subtraction question) In the file room there are 1,200 files. Your supervisor tells you to take out 40 per cent of the files and put them in the next room. How many files should you put into the next room?
   A. 480
   B. 340
   C. 280
   D. None of the above.

4. (Division question) In the file room there are 3,900 files. Your job is to divide the files into 3 equal stacks so that each stack can be put into a separate room. How many files must each stack contain?
   A. 1,333
   B. 1,300
   C. 1, 200
   D. None of the above.

5. (Percentage question) Select the choice which contains two equal amounts.
   A. .25 and 1/3
   B. 33% and 1/4
   C. .15 and 1/10
   D. 20 per cent and 1/5

6. (Multiplication and subtraction question) A supervisor distributes 40 cases to each of his 7 employees. If the supervisor originally had 310 cases, how many cases remain undistributed?
   A. 20
   B. 30
   C. 40
   D. None of the above

7. (Addition, subtraction, division) A large court has 600 employees. On one day during the flu season, 5 per cent of the staff is absent due to sickness and another 5 per cent is out due to scheduled leave. Of those present during the day, 300 are assigned to the Civil Office and the rest of the employees are assigned to the Landlord and Tenant Office. How many employees are assigned to the Landlord and Tenant Office?
   A) 220
   B) 230
   C) 240
   D) 250

Answers:
1. C   2. A   3. A   4. B   5. D   6. B   7. C

CLERICAL ASSISTANT

The following are questions involving forms "usually found in a court setting".

The following table lists Judges and the cases they handled on Monday, June 21, 2015.

Judge	Case Number	Case Type	Disposed	Adjourned
J. Walker	3758/2014	Criminal	YES	---
J. Eckert	4628/2015	Civil	---	YES
J. Williams	3199/2015	Criminal	---	YES
J. Rodriguez	3425/2014	Civil	---	YES
J. Walinsky	3216/2015	Criminal	YES	---
J. Chin	1324/2014	Criminal	YES	---
J. Barnard	4421/2015	Civil	---	YES
J. Chaiken	6564/2015	Civil	---	YES

1. The percentage of cases that were adjourned is:

A. 62.5 %

B. 65 %

C. 30 %

D. None of the above

2. The percentage of criminal cases that were adjourned is:

A. 10 %

B. 12.5 %

C. 25 %

D. None of the above

3. Civil cases comprise what percentage of the total cases listed in the table?:

A. 25 %

B. 50 %

C. 70 %

D. None of the above

4. Criminal cases comprise what percentage of total cases?

A. 25 %

B. 50 %

C. 70 %

D. None of the above

Answers: 1. A   2. C   3. B   4. B

PREPARING WRITTEN MATERIAL

CLERICAL ASSISTANT

7

These questions assess applicants' ability to apply the rules of English grammar and usage, punctuation, and sentence structure. Applicants will be presented with a series of sentences and must select the sentence that best conforms to standard English grammar and usage, punctuation, and sentence structure.*

CLERICAL ASSISTANT

<u>**When answering these types of questions, keep in mind any deviation from standard English grammar, usage, punctuation and sentence structure, including the following:**</u>

1. Is the sentence logical? Is it clear?
2. Are there any misspelled words?
3. Are words used correctly according to their meaning?
4. Are commas, apostrophes, and periods used appropriately?
5. Is the sentence a run-on sentence? Should it be 2 sentences?
6. Is the sample provided not a complete sentence? Is it a sentence fragment?
7. Does the subject (noun) of the sentence agree with the verbs in number (singular / plural?)

For the following ten questions, select the choice that is most correct in accordance with standard English grammar, usage, punctuation and sentence structure.

Examples: (Correct choice is underlined and bold.)

1. A. It is hard to believe that he doesn't want to go to basebal camp. (baseball is misspelled)
   B. It is hard to beleive that he doesn't want to go to baseball camp. (beleive is misspelled)
   C. It is hard to believe that he dont want to go to baseball camp. (dont should be doesn't)
   D. <u>It is hard to believe that he doesn't want to go to baseball camp.</u>

2. A. The following are the tools that you will need. Hammer, nails, and wood glue. (sentence fragments)
   B. The following are the tools that you will need, hammer, nails, and wood glue. (, should be :)
   C. The following are the tools that you will need; Hammer, nails, and wood glue. (; should be :)
   D. <u>The following are the tools that you will need: hammer, nails, and wood glue.</u>

3. A. Both the teacher and the student pay atention to the speaker. (atention should be attention)
   B. Both the teacher and the student pays attention to the speaker. (pays should be pay)
   C. <u>Both the teacher and the student pay attention to the speaker.</u>
   D. Both the teacher and the student pay attention to the speakur. (speakur should be speaker)

4. A. Civil service exams are very fair they ask the same questions of everyone. (run-on sentence)
   B. Civil service exams are very fair. They ask the same questions of everyone (missing period)
   C. Civil service exams are very fair. they ask the same questions of everyone (Capital T not "t")
   D. <u>Civil service exams are very fair. They ask the same questions of everyone.</u>

CLERICAL ASSISTANT

5. A. The principal of the school went to Washington with the students (missing period at end)
   B. The principle of the school went to Washington with the students. (should be principal)
   C The principal of the school went to Washinton with the students. (should be Washington)
   D. The principal of the school went to Washington with the students.

6. A. Someone's who is not moving is stationary. (Someone isn't possessive in this sentence.)
   B. Someone whose is not moving is stationary. (Should be "who is not".)
   C Someone who is not moving is stationary.
   D. Someone who is not moving is stationery. (Should be <u>stationary</u>.)

7. A. There car needed repair. (There should be "their".)
   B. Their car needed repair.
   C There car need repair. ("There" should be "Their" and "need" should be "needs" because car is singular.)
   D. Their car need repair. ("Need" should be "needs" or "needed".)

8. A. He won the race she won the spelling bee. (run-on sentence.)
   B. He won the race she won the spelling be. ("be" should be "bee".)
   C He won the race, she won the spelling bee. (run-on sentence.)
   D. He won the race and she won the spelling bee.

9. **A. He was too happy to speak.**
   B. He was to happy to speak. ("to" should be "too.")
   C He was two happy to speak. ("two means the number "2".)
   D. He was's too happy to speak. ("was's" is not correct usage.)

10. A. The police officers looks tall. ("looks" should be "look" for plural "officers".)
    B. The police officers look tall.
    C The police officer's look tall. ("Officers" should not be possessive.)
    D. The police officers looks tallish. ("tallish" is not common, accepted usage.)

APPLYING FACTS AND INFORMATION TO GIVEN SITUATIONS 8

These questions assess candidates' ability to use the information provided and apply it to a specific situation defined by a given set of facts. Each question contains a brief paragraph which describes a regulation, policy or procedure similar to what a Senior Court Office Assistant may encounter on the job. All of the information needed to answer the questions is contained in the paragraph and in the description of the situation.*

CLERICAL ASSISTANT

Question 1:

PROCEDURE:

Employees must record their attendance daily on their personal time sheet. Upon reporting to work, each employee must "sign-in" by signing the attendance sheet and noting the time of the "signing-in." Employees arriving after their scheduled start time are late and must indicate the time they reported for work and not their regularly scheduled start time. Employees are also required to write their ID number in box 12 and sign the attestation at the bottom of the sheet after their last "sign-out" for that time sheet.

SITUATION:

Helen Edwards, a Court Assistant, travels to work by subway. On Tuesday morning, she leaves her house half an hour earlier than usual, but arrives at work at 9:13 A.M., thirteen minutes after her regularly scheduled sign-in time. The reason for the longer commuting time was a subway delay. Because her assigned Judge had asked her to be in the Part at 9:15 A.M., she did not sign-in, but rushed to her Part and arrived there at 9:15. A.M. Before leaving for the day, at 5:00 P.M., Helen explained the subway delay to her supervisor and signed in (9:00 a.m.) and out (5:00 p.m.) for the day.

1. Based on the above two paragraphs, which of the following statements is not correct?

    A. Helen should have signed in for the day when she arrived and before reporting to her assigned Part.

    B. Helen was thirteen minutes late on Tuesday morning.

    C. Helen reported to her assigned Part on time.

    D. Helen was not late for the day because she left her house half an hour earlier than usual and the subway delays were not within her control.

CLERICAL ASSISTANT

Question 2:

PROCEDURE:

A performance evaluation booklet must be completed for every non judicial employee at least twice a year. The booklets are usually completed by the direct supervisor of the employee who in the evaluation process may consult with other supervisors, including the Chief Clerk of the court. Upon completion of the booklet, the supervisor meets with the employee to review the employee's performance and ratings. Both the employee's weak and strong points are discussed, as well as plans for the employee's professional development. At the end of the discussion, the employee is instructed to sign the last page of the booklet. The signature indicates that the employee has read the booklet but does not necessarily agree with the ratings. An employee who disagrees with the ratings or who wishes to comment on the ratings may do so at the bottom of the last page of the booklet or may attach a statement to the evaluation booklet. The employee receives a copy of the signed booklet for the employee's records and the original is forwarded to central administration of that court.

SITUATION:

Jennifer Benetson, a Court Assistant, met with her supervisor, Robert Finnegan, to discuss her periodic personnel evaluation report. During the meeting, Mr. Finnegan stated that Court Assistant Benetson performed her duties very well and that if her punctuality record did not include six latenesses during the six month period, she would have received an "excellent" rating instead of "above average." Court Assistant Benetson stated that all the latenesses were due to train delays and that her rating should not suffer because of train malfunctions and that she would be speaking with the Chief Clerk about her rating. Because of this, Court Assistant Benetson stated that she would not sign the booklet until she spoke with the Chief Clerk, or unless Mr. Finnegan upgraded the rating.

2. Based on the above two paragraphs, which of the following statements is correct?

    A. Robert Finnegan should not have completed the evaluation booklet before speaking with Court Assistant Benetson and the Chief Clerk.

    B. Court Assistant Benetson supplied a valid reason for not signing the booklet.

    C. Latenesses due to train mechanical malfunctions should be excused by the Chief Clerk.

    D. Court Assistant Benetson must sign the evaluation booklet.

CLERICAL ASSISTANT

Question 3

PROCEDURE:

Civil Court files are public files and may be viewed by any member of the public, including persons who are not parties in the action. A person who wishes to view a file may requisition the file in room 304 where he may view the file under the supervision of appropriate court personnel who are responsible for file safekeeping. A file that is active and stored in a courtroom may be requisitioned in the courtroom. In such cases, the Clerk and Court Officers assigned to the Part are responsible for file safekeeping. Files transported between offices and courtrooms must at all times remain under the direct supervision of court personnel.

SITUATION:

Robert Santiago appears in room 304 and asks to see a file. After reviewing the file, Mr. Santiago asks the Court Assistant in the file room for permission to take the file to Judge Breinman on the eighth floor who has asked to see the file immediately because it impacts on a case which is presently on trial before Judge Breinman.

3. Which of the following is the most correct action for the Court Assistant to take?

   A. The Court Assistant should make sure that Mr. Santiago's name appears in the papers as one of the parties before allowing him to take the file to Judge Breinman.

   B. In addition to "A," the Court Assistant should also make certain that the file is an active file before allowing Mr. Santiago to take the file to Judge Breinman.

   C. Inform Mr. Santiago that he may take the file because Civil Court files are public files.

   D. Confirm with Judge Breinman or his Court Officer that they wish to see the file before having court personnel take the file to Judge Breinman.

CLERICAL ASSISTANT

Answers for questions 1 – 3:

1. The answer is "D. Helen was not late for the day because she left her house half an hour earlier than usual and the subway delays were not within her control.
(This statement is **not correct** because this excuse does not change the requirement that she sign-in at the time of arrival to work.)

2. The answer is "D. Court Assistant Benetson must sign the evaluation booklet."
(The procedure states, "At the end of the discussion, the employee is instructed to sign the last page of the booklet. The signature indicates that the employee has read the booklet but does not necessarily agree with the ratings.")

3. The answer is "D. Confirm with Judge Breinman or his Court Officer that they wish to see the file before having court personnel take the file to Judge Breinman."
(The procedure states, "Files transported between offices and courtrooms must remain under the direct supervision of court personnel.")

CODING AND DECODING 9

These questions assess applicants' ability to use written sets of directions to encode information and use coded information for keeping records.

Applicants will be presented with a table of coded information and then be asked to apply a set of coding rules to encode information accurately.*

CLERICAL ASSISTANT

Answer questions 1 - 10 based on the tables below which contain employee information and codes.

Employee Codes

Last Name, First Name	Court Where Assigned	County of Residence	Pension Tier	Union Representation	Health Insurance
Johnson, Alice	F	W	4	2	4
Weinstein, Barry	R	D	4	5	3
Rodriguez, Charles	T	W	2	6	1
Chin, Daniel	S	M	4	1	2
Ruggiero, Ryan	R	Q	3	3	4
Molson, Grace	C	B	6	6	1
Braker, Leonora	F	K	6	2	3
Furstein, Janice	X	K	5	3	4

Employee Codes Explanation

Court Where Assigned	County of Residence	Pension Tier
C = Civil (Lower) T = County Court X = Civil (Supreme) F = Family R = Criminal (Lower) S = Surrogates	K = Kings Q = Queens W = Westchester D = Dutchess M = Richmond B = Bronx	2 = Tier 2 3 = Tier 3 4 = Tier 4 5 = Tier 5 6 = Tier 6
Union Representation	Health Insurance	Codes are in this order: Court Where Employed, County of Residence, Pension Tier, Union, Health Insurance Example: CB353 (Civil (Lower), Bronx, Tier 3, HDUTS, NYAWN)
1 = FHAA 2 = DJFIA 3 = CONYP 4 = CIBSA 5 = HDUTS 6 = EADRS	1 = NYEPA 2 = ACRBD 3 = NYAWN 4 = BTHSD 5 = ACECA	

CLERICAL ASSISTANT

1. What is (are) the name(s) of the employee(s) who have signed-up with the CONYP union?

A. Johnson and Braker

B. Braker and Furstein

C. Furstein and Ruggiero

D. Johnson and Furstein

2. How many people are represented by the EADRS union?

A. 4

B. 3

C. 2

D. 1

3. Which of the following unions was not selected by any of the employees listed in the preceding list?

A. DJFIA

B. CIBSA

C. FHAA

D. CONYP

4. What is the total number of employees that live in the Bronx or Westchester?

A. 2

B. 4

C. 5

D. 3

5. The two courts that each have two new employees assigned are ____.

A. Civil (Lower) Court and Civil (Supreme) Court

B. Family Court and Surrogates Court

C. County Court and Family Court

D. Family Court and Criminal (Lower) Court

6. A new employee is scheduled to start work today at the Family Court. He lives in Richmond County and is in Pension Tier 6. He has chosen to be represented by the CONYP union and has signed up with ACECA Health Insurance. Based on the preceding, which of the following is his correct employee code?

A. FM535

B. FR365

C. RM635

D. FM635

CLERICAL ASSISTANT

7. Another employee is also scheduled to start working at the Supreme (Civil) Court. He presently lives in Westchester County, but is thinking of moving to a different county, perhaps Dutchess. He is in Tier 6 pension system and is already registered with the ACRBD Health Insurers. He has selected EADRS as the union which will represent him. Based on the preceding, which of the following is his correct employee code?

A. WX626

B. XW662

C. WC626

D. XC662

8. A new employee calls the administration office of the Civil Court (Lower), where you are assigned as a Clerical Assistant. She states that her Employee Code is CK642. She signed-up for health insurance, but does not remember the name of the Health Insurance company. She asks if you would please look it up. Based on the Employee Code provided by the new employee and the employee codes tables, you correctly determine that her health insurance plan is_____.

A. NYAWN

B. ACECA

C. BTHSD

D. ACRB

9. A new employee is assigned to Criminal (Lower) Court and she lives in Richmond County. The first two letters of her employee code are_____.

A. CM

B. RC

C. RM

D. CR

10. Which of the following two employee codes are for employees that are in Pension Tier 4?

A. RQ3CONYP4 and XK5CONYP4

B. SM4FHAA2 and RQ3CONYP4

C. RQ3CONYP4 and SM4FHAA2

D. SM4FHAA2 and FW4DJFIA4

Answers 1 - 10

1. C. Furstein and Ruggiero
2. C. 2
3. B. CIBSA
4. D. 3 (1 + 2 = 3)
5. D. Family Court and Criminal (Lower) Court Courts F and R
6. D. FM635
7. B. XW662
8. D. ACRB
9. C. RM
10. D. SM4FHAA2 and FW4DJFIA4

CLERICAL ASSISTANT

Answer questions 11 - 20 based on the tables below which contain employee information and codes.

Case Codes

Name of Respondent (Defendant)	Court	County	Year Case Filed	Type of Case	Disposition
Reynolds	1	4	4	1	4
Tumberino	2	2	4	6	3
Wallace	3	1	2	1	1
Ming	1	3	4	2	2
Vorlotas	2	6	3	4	4
Williams	1	3	6	2	1
Berger	2	2	6	3	3
Trammer	2	1	5	3	4

Case Codes Explanation

Court	County	Year Case Filed
1 = Criminal 2 = Family 3 = County	1 = Kings 2 = Queens 3 = Westchester 4 = Dutchess 5 = Richmond 6 = Bronx	1 = 2015 3 = 2016 4 = 2017 5 = 2018 6 = 2019
Type of Case	**Disposition**	
1 = Misdemeanor 2 = Violation 3 = Juvenile Delinquent 4 = Person In Need of Supervision 5 = Abuse 6 = Family Offense	1 = Dismissed 2 = ACD 3 = Probation 4 = Judgment 5 = Pending	Codes are in this order: Court, County, Year Case Filed, Type of Case, Disposition Example: 14414 (Criminal Court, Dutchess County, Case Filed 2017, Misdemeanor Case, Disposed By Judgment)

CLERICAL ASSISTANT

11. One of the persons listed in the preceding "Case Codes" table was a defendant in a criminal case in Westchester County during the year 2019. The charge was a violation which was ultimately dismissed. Which of the following four persons has a case code that fits this set of facts?

A. Ming

B. Reynolds

C. Vorlotas

D. Williams

12. What was the "Year Case Filed" for defendant Ming?

A. 2016

B. 2017

C. 2018

D. 2019

13. The cases of respondents Tumberino and Vorlotas were assigned case codes. Tumberino's assigned case code is 22463 and Vorlotas' case code is 26344. Both cases were disposed by Probation. Which of the following four statements is true?

A. Both case codes are correct.

B. Vorlotas' case code is the only one that is correct.

C. Tumerino's case code is the only one that is correct.

D. Both case codes are not correct.

14. Which of the following statements is correct?

A. Berger's case was disposed by Judgment.

B. There is one ADC disposition.

C. There is one disposition that is marked Pending.

D. The type of disposition with the greatest number of dispositions is code 4.

15. Which court has the greatest number of cases?

A. Criminal Court

B. Family Court

C. Surrogates Court

D. Family Court

CLERICAL ASSISTANT

16. The case code for a person with a Family Offense case in 2018 Family Court (Kings County) that was dismissed is _____.

A. 31516

B. 25611

C. 12561

D. 21561

17. Which disposition is not listed in the "Disposition" column of the Case Codes Table?

A. 2

B. 2

C. 4

D. 5

18. Which year had the greatest number of cases filed?

A. 2018

B. 2017

C. 2016

D. 2015

19. Which county did not have any cases filed?

A. Westchester County

B. Dutchess County

C. Kings County

D. Richmond County

20. The name of the respondent in the Queens County Family Court case (Family Offense) filed in 2017 and that was disposed by Probation is _____.

A. Vorlota

B. Williams

C. Berger

D. Tumberino

Answers 11 - 20

11. D. Williams

12. B. 2017

13. C. Tumberino's case code is the only one that is correct.

14. D. The type of disposition with the greatest number of dispositions is code 4.

15. D. Family Court (Code 2, with 4 cases)

16. D. 21561

17. D. 5 (Pending)

18. B. 2017 (Code 4)

19 D. Richmond County (Code 5)

20. D. Tumberino (Code 22463)

CLERICAL ASSISTANT

PRACTICE TEST 10

Try to take this test (untimed) and at one sitting. The actual test may be 3-4 hours long. After the test, review any questions or types of questions that you found difficult. (Practice makes perfect!)

PRACTICE TEST

1. On Monday 360 new employees started working for the NYS Unified Court System. Of those new employees, 40 per cent of them live within New York City. The number of employees who live within New York City is:
A. 124   B. 144   C. 164   D. None of the above

2. In family court, Part A, there were 60 cases scheduled. In Part B there were 87 cases scheduled. In the entire family court there are a total of 289 cases scheduled. How many cases are scheduled in parts other than A and B?
A. 124   B. 144   C. 147   D. None of the above

3. In the file room there are 900 files. Your supervisor tells you to take out 20 per cent of the files and put them in the next room. How many files should you put into the next room?
A. 18   B. 108   C. 180   D. None of the above

4. In the file room there are 3,640 files. Your job is to divide the files into four equal stacks so that each stack can be put into a separate room. How many files must each stack contain?
A. 91   B. 901   C. 910   D. None of the above

5. Select the best answer: The choice which contains the closest two equal amounts is:
A. .30 and 1/3   B. 33.333% and 1/3   C. .10 and 1/11   D. 22 per cent and 1/5

CLERICAL ASSISTANT

6. A supervisor distributes for processing 30 cases to each of his six employees. If the supervisor originally had 200 cases, how many cases remain undistributed?

A. 24 B. 20 C. 180 D. None of the above

7. On Monday 84 phone inquiries were handled by the Special Term Office. On Tuesday 93 telephone inquiries were handled by the Special Term Office. If the total number of phone inquiries handled by the Special Term Office for Monday, Tuesday and Wednesday were 283, how many telephone inquiries were handled on Wednesday?

A. 96 B. 106 C. 116 D. None of the above

8. A total of 450 cases were processed on Monday. Of those cases, 150 were processed by James Wilkins. The remainder of the cases were processed equally by Lorraine Hawkins and Jane Chin. How many cases did Lorraine Hawkins and Jane Chin each process?

A. 100 B. 125 C. 300 D. 150

9. The Judgments supervisor hands each of his nine employee 32 judgments to process. The total number of judgments which the supervisor handed out is:

A. 32 B. 9 C. 287 D. 288

10. An examination had 50 questions, with each correct answer worth 2 per cent of the final score. Kevin answered 42 questions correctly. His final score on the test is:

A. 42 B. 48 C. 80 D. 84

11. A court receives 270 cases for processing. If one employee can process 45 cases a day, how many days will that employee need to process all the 270 cases?

A. 5 B. 6 C. 7 D. None of the above

12. Adam processed 40 cases. Bob processed 50 cases. Cynthia processed 55 cases. David processed 55 cases. The average number of cases processed by Adam. Bob, Cynthia and David is:

A. 45 B. 50 C. 55 D. 54

13. The Supreme Court in Kings County received 1040 cases in one week. Because of the large number of cases received, twenty per cent were sent to the NYC Civil Court for processing. How many case did the Supreme Court in Kings County send to the NYC Civil Court?

A. 208 B. 20 C. 200 D. None of the above

CLERICAL ASSISTANT

14. Which of the following is 1/4 of 10,860?
A. 2715
B. 2751
C. 2710
D. None of the above

15. Choose the best answer: Ten court officers are assigned to security posts. Twenty court officers are assigned to courtrooms. If the total court officers assigned, what per cent is assigned to security posts?
A. 33.333 per cent
B. 25 per cent
C. 30%
D. None of the above

For questions 16 - 20 below, compare the three sets of information and mark your answer sheet with the correct choice, as follows:

A. Only the second and third sets are exactly alike.
B. Only the first and third sets are exactly alike.
C. None of the sets are exactly alike.
D. All three sets are exactly alike.

16.
C.R. Ed Hymowitz
SS# 892-45-8193
Family Court (1837)
372-38 129th Street
FCA 3 (192.37)

C.R. Ed Hymowitz
SS# 892-45-8193
Family Court (1837)
372-38 129th Street
FCA 3 (192.73)

C.R. Ed Hymowitz
SS# 892-45-8193
Family Court (1837)
372-38 129th Street
FCA 3 (192.37)

17.
J. James Holbrook
C.O. Brannigan, H.
765429759-38729A
Part 5, Part 8
KCV 62849/01

J. James Holbrook
C.O. Brannigan, H.
765429759-38729
Part 5, Part 8
KCV 62849/01

J. James Holbrook
C.O. Brannigan, H.
765429759-38729A
Part 2, Part 8
KCV 62849/01

18.
HC2948.KA83214
Kerns, Leonard
CPLR and FCA
C98621/8398/25
Doubleday, NY (99)

HC2948.KA83214
Kerns, Leonard
CPLR and FCA
C98621/8398/25
Doubleday, NY (99)

HC2948.KA83214
Kerns, Leonard
CPLR and FCA
C98621/8398/25
Doubleday, NY (99)

19.
Civ Procedure Law
CPL 325.46, a & d
Dickerson, Evelyn
9/26/99, 2/16/01
SCK 10385/01

Civ Procedure Law
CPL 325.46, a & b
Dickerson, Evelyn
9/26/99, 2/16/01
SCK 10385/01

Civ Procedure Law
CPL 325.46, a & b
Dickerson, Evelyn
9/26/99, 2/16/01
SCK 10385/01

CLERICAL ASSISTANT

20. Jenkins, Richard
    NY Laws and Rules
    NY7349.72 (c)
    USA Med. Mal.
    USACL01/6927342

    Jenkinz, Richard
    NY Laws and Rules
    NY7349.72 (c)
    USA Med. Mal.
    USACL01/6927342

    Jenkins, Richard
    NY Laws and Rules
    NY7349.72 (c)
    USA Med. Mal.
    USACL01/6927342

For questions 21 - 30, compare the three sets of information and mark your answer sheet with the correct choice, as follows:

A. Only the first and second sets are exactly alike.
B. None of the sets are exactly alike.
C. Only the second and third sets are exactly alike.
D. All three sets are exactly alike.

21. Kiefer, Mohammud
    HGSN90274365
    Urly & Devry, P.C.
    Sept. 27, 1998
    Civ01/32761

    HGSN90274365
    Kiefer, Mohammud
    Sept. 27, 1998
    Civ01/32761
    Urly & Devry, P.C.

    Urly & Devry, P.C.
    Sept. 27, 1998
    Civ01/321761
    Kiefer, Mohammud
    HGSN90274365

22. OCR Peter Wong
    Pt. 21 (9:25 AM)
    J. Larry Oberman
    SCK7823/98 (38)

    Pt. 21 (9:25 AM)
    OCR Peter Wong
    SCK7823/98 (38)
    J. Larry Oberman

    J. Larry Oberman
    SCK7823/98 (38)
    OCR Peter Wong
    Pt. 21 (9:25 AM)

23. SC (NY) 111 Centre
    7 Magnetometers
    Sgt. K. Elvison
    S#: 869436829-38

    Sgt. K. Elvison
    S#: 869438629-38
    SC (NY) 111 Centre
    7 Magnetometers

    S#: 869436829-38
    SC (NY) 111 Centre
    7 Magnetometers
    Sgt. K. Elvisson

24. Hayt and Wryer, PC
    26 Court St. 17D
    Wed. 7/28/01 9AM
    Pt. 18C (J. Parsons)

    Hayt and Wryer, PC
    Wed. 7/28/01 9AM
    26 Court St. 17D
    Pt. 18C (J. Parson)

    Hayt and Wryer, PC
    Wed. 7/28/01 9AM
    Pt. 18C (J. Parson)
    26 Court St. 17D

25. CPL389.2671(B)
    37538765-498
    Peters, Hannah
    FCA, CPLR (a)

    37538765-498
    Peters, Hannah
    CPL389.2671(B)
    FCA, CPLR (a)

    FCA, CPLR (a)
    CPL389.2671(B)
    Peters, Hannah
    37538765-498

CLERICAL ASSISTANT

26. JLK:03542987392
    Law Publ., Inc.
    1/13/02 (Pt. 2)
    LV65921.45629

    Law Publ., Inc.
    JLK:03542987392
    LV65921.45629
    1/13/02 (Pt. 5)

    1/13/02 (Pt. 5)
    LV65921.45629
    JLK:03542987392
    Law Publ., Inc.

27. ID 25649/01
    J. Ed Tremont
    293 E. 28th Ave.
    L2897369.7231

    293 E. 28th Ave.
    L2897369.7231
    ID 52649/01
    J. Ed Tremont

    L2897369.7231
    J. Ed Tremont
    293 E. 28th St.
    ID 25649/01

28. CO Lorna J. Kim
    CR Mark S. Lipsky
    S2839.82010251
    DCAS PON7189

    CO Lorna J. Kim
    S2839.82010251
    DCAS PON7189
    CR Mark S. Lipsky

    DCAS PON7189
    CR Mark S. Lipsky
    CO Lorna J. Kim
    S283982010251

29. Fleming V ZBR
    CFK125712/01
    J. Salamin, R.
    PC73529.2819

    J. Salamin, R.
    PC73529.2819
    CFK125721/01
    Fleming V ZBR

    PC73529.2819
    Fleming V ZBR
    J. Salamin, R.
    CFK125721/01

30. SS876092.782
    DN7389/199
    7/24/99 & 12/3/01
    Durston, Nicholas

    7/24/99 & 12/3/01
    SS876092.782
    DN7389/199
    Durston, Nicholas

    SS876092.782
    DN7389/199
    7/24/99 & 12/3/01
    Durston, Nicholas

For questions 31 - 35, compare the three sets of information and mark your answer sheet with the correct choice, as follows:
A. Only the first and second sets are exactly alike.
B. None of the sets are exactly alike.
C. Only the second and third sets are exactly alike.
D. All three sets are exactly alike.

31. *FCA and CPL Law*
    JBN538549276
    ASF638.B293
    Ruljower, Erik

    ASF638.B293
    Ruljower, Erik
    JBN538549276
    FCA and CPL Law

    FCA and CPL Law
    JBN538549276
    Ruljower, Erik
    ASF638.B293

CLERICAL ASSISTANT

32. ALBERMARLE RD. 16
PET. KYLE ROUTER
127 LIV. ST. 7F-252
SEC8273955.4629

PET. KYLE ROUTER
127 Liv. St. 7F-252
Albermarle Rd. 16
SEC8273955.4629

127 Liv. St. 7F-252
Albermarl Rd. 16
Pet. Kyle Router
SEC8273955.4629

33. *425-52 W. 129 Ave.*
Priority 7F97312
Aided K01/078-9
OSHA 37485726

AIDED K01/078-9
OSHA 37485726
425-52 W. 129 AVE.
PRIORITY 7F93712

Priority 7F93712
Aided K01/078-9
425-52 W. 129 Ave.
OSHA 37485726

34. Fredericks, Bill
Apex BP, Inc.
Criminal Law
X93717197321

Apex BP, Inc.
Criminal Law
Fredericks, Bill
X93717197321

X937171197321
Fredericks, Bill
Apex BP, Inc.
Criminal Law

CLERICAL ASSISTANT

Questions 36 - 45:

Below is a list of employees, the date each was hired, employee ID number and department.
First, prepare 4 lists of the employees in
1. alphabetical order by last name
2. Employee Number (numerical order)
3. date hired order
4. department order (alphabetical order of departments with alphabetical list of employees within that department).

After preparing the above lists, answer the 10 questions that follow. (You will not be graded on the lists. You will only be graded on your answers to the 10 questions).

NAME	DATE HIRED	EMPLOYEE NUMBER	DEPARTMENT
Worth, Jules	5/17/2003	66892	Judgments
Jordan, James	6/3/1987	88234	Warrants
Grodin, Bill	3/4/1978	34889	Small Claims
Patterson, Leonard	8/8/1998	00273	Judgments
Aikens, Kim	5/5/1983	45999	Special Term
Yard, William	2/9/2002	54908	Landlord and Tenant
Osgood, Jill	5/6/1988	37890	Special Term
Dartmouth, Kim	6/1/1984	18767	Calendar
Heniken, Eleanor	5/6/2002	99012	Warrants
Quigly, Norma	6/5/1976	82098	Special Term
Roller, Francine	3/7/2004	34567	Judgments
Zales, David	2/2/2003	51435	Calendar
Vanguard, George	5/4/1974	88657	Calendar
Dundee, Robert	7/5/1997	35912	Landlord and Tenant
Minkin, Lena	8/4/1982	87777	General Clerk
Feinstein, Pat	4/3/2003	29329	Special Term
Brinks, Sam	3/5/2001	81432	Landlord and Tenant
Joones, Erik	4/2/1988	77953	Judgments
United, Frank	2/7/2002	32598	Judgments
Paline, Thomas	5/2/1996	63999	Warrants
Wonkin, Paul	9/9/1987	44876	General Clerk
Chin, Robert	2/2/1995	34354	Small Claims
Kevany, Pamela	6/4/1977	96345	Judgments
Ericson, Vivian	8/4/1999	89876	Special Term
Battle, James	4/1/1986	10241	Appeals

CLERICAL ASSISTANT

Examples of the completed worksheets are as follows

<u>Alphabetical order by last name</u>

a Aikens	b Battle Brinks	c Chin	d Dartmouth Dundee
e Ericson	f Feinstein	g Grodin	h Heniken
i	j Joones Jordan	k Kevany	l
m Minkin	n	o Osgood	p Paline Patterson
q Quigly	r Roller	s	t
u United	v Vanguard	w Wonkin Worth	x

y   Yard   z   Zales

1. Aikens
2. Battle
3. Brinks
4. Chin
5. Dartmouth
6. Dundee
7. Ericson
8. Feinstein
9. Grodin
10. Heniken
11. Joones
12. Jordan
13. Kevany
14. Minikin
15. Osgood
16. Paline
17. Patterson
18. Quigly
19. Roller
20. United
21. Vanguard
22. Wonkin
23. Worth
24. Yard
25. Zales

CLERICAL ASSISTANT

Employee Number (numerical order)

0-10,000	10,001-20,000	20,001-30,000	30,001-40,000	40,001-50,000
00273	10241 18767	29329	32958 34354 34567 34889 35912 37890	44876 45999

50,001-60,000	60,001-70,000	70,001-80,000	80,001-90,000	90,001-100,000
51435 54908	63999 66892	77953	81432 82098 87777 88234 88657 89876	96345 99012

1. 00273
2. 10241
3. 18767
4. 29329
5. 32958
6. 34354
7. 34567
8. 34889
9. 35912
10. 37890
11. 44876
12. 45999
13. 51435
14. 54908
15. 63999
16. 66892
17. 77953
18. 81432
19. 82098
20. 87777
21. 88234
22. 88657
23. 89876
24. 96345
25. 99012

CLERICAL ASSISTANT

Date Hired Order

1970s	1980s	1990s	2000s
5-4-74	8-4-82	2-2-95	3-5-2001
6-5-76	5-5-83	5-2-96	2-7-2002
6-4-77	6-1-84	7-5-97	2-9-2002
3-4-78	4-1-86	8-8-98	5-6-2002
	6-3-87	8-4-99	2-2-2003
	9-9-87		4-3-2003
	4-2-88		5-17-2003
	5-6-88		3-7-2004

1. 5-4-74
2. 6-5-76
3. 6-4-77
4. 3-4-78
5. 8-4-82
6. 5-5-83
7. 6-1-84
8. 4-1-86
9. 6-3-87
10. 9-9-87
11. 4-2-88
12. 5-6-88
13. 2-2-95
14. 5-2-96
15. 7-5-97
16. 8-8-98
17. 8-4-99
18. 3-5-2001
19. 2-07-2002
20. 2-9-2002
21. 5-6-2002
22. 2-2-2003
23. 4-3-2003
24. 5-17-2003
25. 3-7-2004

CLERICAL ASSISTANT

Department order (and alphabetical order of employees in alphabetized departments)

Appeals	
Battle	
Calendar	
Dartmouth	
Vanguard	
Zales	
General Clerk	
Minikin	
Wonkin	
Judgments	
Joones	
Kevany	
Patterson	
Roller	
United	
Worth	
Landlord & Tenant	
Brinks	
Dundee	
Yard	
Small Claims	
Chin	
Grodin	
Special Term	
Aikens	
Ericson	
Feinstein	
Osgood	
Quigly	
Warrants	
Henikin	
Jordan	
Paline	

1. Appeals   Battle
2. Calendar   Dartmouth
3.   Vanguard
4.   Zales
5. General Clerk   Miniken
6.   Wonkin
7. Judgments   Joones
8.   Kevany
9.   Patterson
10.   Roller
11.   United
12.   Worth
13. Landlord and Tenant   Brinks
14.   Dundee
15.   Yard
16. Small Claims   Chin
17.   Grodin
18. Special Term   Aikens
19.   Ericson
20.   Feinstein
21.   Osgood
22.   Quigly
23. Warrants   Henikin
24.   Jordan
25.   Paline

CLERICAL ASSISTANT

36. The tenth name in the Last Name Alphabetical File is:
    A. Fernstein   B. Grodin   C. Heniken   D. Joones

37. The twenty-second name in the Last Name Alphabetical File is:
    A. Wonkir   B. Vanguard   C. Worth   D. Wonkin

38. Which of the following four statements is not correct?
    A. Zales is the last name in the Last Name Alphabetical File.
    B. Feinstein is the eighth name in the Last Name Alphabetical File.
    C. Dundee is the sixth name in the Last Name Alphabetical file.
    D. Jordan is the fourteenth name in the Last Name Alphabetical File.

39. The employee whose hired date is listed number 6 on the chronological date hired list is:
    A. Minkin, Lena   B. Aikens, Kim   C. Dartmouth, Jim   D. None of the above

40. The name of the employee whose employee number is listed number 18 on the chronological employee number list is ____:
    A. Kevany, Pamela
    B. Brinks, Sam
    C. Jameson, Erik
    D. Vanguard, George

41. Employee Robert Chin's employee number is listed number ___ on the list of employee numbers.
    A. 6   B. 7   C. 8   D. 9

42. The employee whose employee number is number 10 on the chronological list of employee numbers works in the ___ department.
    A. General Clerk   B. Special Term   C. Calendar   D. Small Claims

43. Employee number 82098 is listed number ___ on the chronological list of employee numbers.
    A. 19   B. 20   C. 18   D. 21

44. The name of the employee that is listed last on the chronological list of employee numbers is named:
    A. Battle, James   B. Heniken, Eleanor   C. Worth, Jules   D. Zales, David

45. The number of employees assigned to the Judgments department is:
    A. 4   B. 5   C. 7   D. None of the above

For questions 46 - 60, read the paragraph and then choose the word which best fits in each of the underlined spaces.

CLERICAL ASSISTANT

A person of average __46__ cannot move the chair. The reason for this is that the chair weighs over 200 pounds. Also, a person of average __47__ cannot see over the wall. The chair and the wall, therefore, are in __48__ of ADA requirements and therefore must be corrected to avoid a fine. The federal inspector will __49__ in 60 days to inspect the site once again.

46. A. height   B. temperament   C. weight   D. strength
47. A. strength   B. weight   C. temperament   D. height
48. A. concurrence   B. agreement   C. tandem   D. violation
49. A. sojourn   B. respect   C. return   D. detour

The account of the witness was __50__ to believe. The reason for this is that there was no light in the room and therefore no way for him to see who broke the vase. The fingerprint analysis is a much __51__ indicator of who is guilty. Fingerprints are unique and when __52__ to those on the broken pieces, provide reasonable cause to believe who broke the vase.

50. A. easy   B. likely   C. hard   D. not
51. A. less   B. more   C. worse   D. better
52. A. differed   B. differentiated   C. matched   D. dissolved

The new Court Officer and the young litigant __53__ going to be here tomorrow morning. Please have the subpoenaed records ready for them. The attorneys __54__ also authorized to see them. Copies may be made by them. However, the original documents may not be __55__ out of the record room.

53. A. is   B. was   C. are   D. isn't
54. A. is   B. are   C. was   D. aren't
55. A. brought   B. taking   C. taken   D. takened

Perhaps one indicator of truly enlightened court administration is __56__ on quality public service. Lacking the historic "profit motive" for emphasizing quality public service, the enlightened court administrator does so __57__ for the public good than any financial gain.

56. A. avoidance   B. seeking   C. diminishing   D. emphasis
57. A. less   B. because   C. more   D. seeking

Alternative dispute resolution (ADR) is a __58__ by which parties in a dispute seek resolution of their dispute without a court trial. Two methods used in ADR are mediation and arbitration. Unless otherwise agreed to, parties __59__ participate in mediation and arbitration do not give up __60__ right to submit their controversy to a court for trial.

58. A. procedures   B. process   C. attempts   D. prescriptions
59. A. which   B. whom   C. who   D. too
60. A. his   B. their   C. her   D. your

CLERICAL ASSISTANT

The following table applies to questions 71-75. Before answering the questions, complete the partially filled-in table based on the partial information provided.

Case Activity	SUMMARY OF CASES Terms 1 - 5					
	Term 1	Term 2	Term 3	Term 4	Term 5	Total Number of Cases
Adjourned	6		2	5	3	20
Defaulted	2	4	3	1		15
Dismissed	3	1	3	2	3	
Settled - with money award	4	6	4		5	
Settled - with no money award		1	3	2	2	11
Total Number of Cases On Calendar	18	16		17		84

61. What is the total number of cases adjourned during Term 3?
    A. 20 B. 16 C. 17 D. 18

62. What is the total number of dismissed cases?
    A. 10 B. 11 C. 12 D. 13

63. What is the total number of cases "settled - with money award" and "settled - with no money award"?
    A. 35 B. 36 C. 37 D. 38

64. What is the total number of "defaulted" and "dismissed" cases?
    A. 26 B. 27 C. 28 D. 29

65. Which term had the least number of cases on the calendar?
    A. Term 2 B. Term 3 C. Term 4 D. Term 5

CLERICAL ASSISTANT

Using the information in table 1, complete tables 2, 3 and 4, and then answer questions 66-85 based on the information in tables 1 - 4.

DAILY CASE LOG						Table 1
Monday - Friday						
Part	Case Type	Date Filed	Day Appeared On Court Calendar	Case Status	Money Award	Fine
Part 1	Civil	3/16/98	Monday	Dismissed	X	
Part 2	Civil	7/9/97	Monday	Settled	X	
Part 1	Criminal	5/16/98	Monday	Trial completed		$5,000
Part 3	Civil	3/21/99	Monday	Settled	X	
Part 4	Criminal	9/24/00	Monday	Trial completed		X
Part 5	Civil	4/13/97	Tuesday	Dismissed	X	
Part 6	Criminal	12/24/00	Tuesday	Trial completed		$3,000
Part 7	Civil	2/7/96	Tuesday	Settled	$7,500	
Part 1	Criminal	5/21/01	Tuesday	Trial completed		X
Part 3	Criminal	5/21/01	Tuesday	Adjourned		X
Part 6	Civil	7/26/98	Tuesday	Settled	$21,500	
Part 5	Civil	2/15/97	Wednesday	Settled	X	
Part 4	Civil	12/9/98	Wednesday	Settled	$5,400	
Part 5	Civil	3/16/97	Wednesday	Defaulted	X	
Part 5	Civil	4/22/98	Wednesday	Adjourned	X	
Part 1	Criminal	4/12/99	Thursday	Trial completed		$3,000
Part 6	Civil	4/14/99	Thursday	Adjourned	X	
Part 3	Civil	6/24/98	Thursday	Settled	$2,400	
Part 4	Civil	3/7/97	Thursday	Dismissed	X	
Part 5	Civil	1/26/98	Friday	Defaulted	X	
Part 3	Criminal	4/21/98	Friday	Adjourned		X
Part 1	Civil	5/26/96	Friday	Settled	$1,500	

CLERICAL ASSISTANT

SUMMARY OF CASES — Table 2
Monday - Friday

Case Activity	Monday	Tuesday	Wednesday	Thursday	Friday	Total Number of Cases
Adjourned						
Defaulted						
Dismissed						
Settled - with money award						
Settled - with no money award						
Trial completed - with fine						
Trial completed - with no fine						
Total Number of Cases On Calendar						

Table 3 — SUMMARY OF CASES (BY YEAR FILED)
Monday - Friday

Year Filed	Monday	Tuesday	Wed.	Thursday	Friday	Total Number of Cases
1996						
1997						
1998						
1999						
2000						
2001						
Total Number of Cases						

CLERICAL ASSISTANT

SUMMARY OF CASES (BY PART)   Table 4
Monday - Friday

Part	Adjourned	Dismissed	De-faulted	Settled - with no money award	Settled - with money award	Trial completed- no fine	Trial completed - with fine	Total Cases
1								
2								
3								
4								
5								
6								
7								
Total								

66. How many cases were filed during 1997?
A. 4   B. 5   C. 6   D. 7

67. How many cases were settled on Tuesday and Wednesday with a money award?
A. 1   B. 2   C. 3   D. 4

68. What is the total number of cases adjourned or defaulted on Wednesday?
A. 1   B. 2   C. 3   D. 4

69. How many cases were settled on Monday and Tuesday with no money award?
A. 3   B. 2   C. 1   D. 0

70. What is the total number of cases adjourned by Part 1 and Part 5?
A. 1   B. 2   C. 3   D. 4

71. Which Part has the greatest number of adjourned cases?
A. Part 6   B. Part 4   C. Part 3   D. Part 5

72. Which Parts have more cases "Settled - with money award" than they have cases "Settled - with no money award?"
A. Parts 1, 4, 6 and 7   B. Parts 1, 6 and 7   C. Parts 4, 6 and 7   D. Part 1, 4 and 7

73. What is the total number of cases "Settled-with no money award" and "Settled-with money award"?
A. 8   B. 9   C. 10   D. 11

CLERICAL ASSISTANT

74. The total number of cases filed in 1996 and 1998 is?
A. 12
B. 13
C. 11
D. 10

75. Which Part has the greatest number of defaulted cases?
A. Part 5
B. Part 4
C. Part 3
D. Part 2

76. The total of cases "Settled - with money award" exceeded the total of cases "Settled - with no money award" by:
A. 3
B. 4
C. 2
D. 6

77. Total number of cases Dismissed and Defaulted exceeded the total number of cases adjourned by:
A. 1
B. 2
C. 3
D. 4

78. Choose the best answer: Cases filed in 1996 appeared on the calendar on which days?
A. Monday
B. Tuesday
C. Thursday and Friday
D. Tuesday and Friday

79. What is the total number of cases filed in 1998 and 1997?
A. 9
B. 10
C. 12
D. 13

80. The three Parts which had more than three cases on the calendar were:
A. Parts 1, 5 and 7
B. Parts 1, 3 and 5
C. Parts 3, 5 and 6
D. Parts 2, 5 and 7

81. The Part which had the greatest number of case "Trial completed - with fine" was:
A. Part 1
B. Part 2
C. Part 3
D. Part 4

82. The number of "Trials completed - with fine" exceeds the number of "Trials completed - no fine" by:
A. 4
B. 3
C. 2
D. 1

83. The total number of cases Monday - Friday was:
A. 6
B. 22
C. 8
D. 9

84. The year in which exactly 3 cases were filed is:
A. 1998
B. 1999
C. 2000
D. 1996

85. The total number of settled cases is:
A. 6
B. 7
C. 8
D. 9

For questions 86 - 90, select the choice that is most correct in accordance with standard English grammar, usage, punctuation and sentence structure.

CLERICAL ASSISTANT

86. A. The applicant scored high because he studied dilligently.
    B. The applicant scored high because he studied diligently.
    C. The applicant scored high because he studied dilegently.
    D. The applicant scored high because he studied diliggently.

87. A. The argument was between John, Eleanor and William.
    B. The argument was among John, Eleanor and William.
    C. The arguments was between John, Eleanor and William.
    D. The arguments is between John, Eleanor and William.

88. A. Its the best way to study.
    B. Its the best ways to study.
    C. It's the best way to study.
    D. Its' the best way to study.

89. A. The exam was difficult the proctor was young.
    B. The exam was difficult --the proctor was young.
    C. The exam was difficult and the proctor was young.
    D. The exam was difficult / the proctor was young.

90. A. The bag contained the following pencils, pens, erasers and a ruler.
    B. The bag contained the following; pencils, pens, erasers and a ruler.
    C. The bag contained the following items pencils, pens, erasers and a ruler.
    D. The bag contained the following: pencils, pens, erasers and a ruler.

Questions 91-95

PROCEDURE: (Processing of passport application)

As directed by public law 106-119 and 22 CFR 51.27 effective July 2, 2001: To submit an application for a child under age 14, both parents or the child's legal guardian(s) must appear and present evidence of the child's US citizenship and evidence of the child's relationship to parents/guardians, and parental identification. As directed by regulation 22 CFR 51 effective February 1, 2004, each minor child applying for a passport must appear in person.

For a person who is 16 years of age or older, the passport processing fee is $55, the application execution fee is $30, and the security surcharge is $12. The passport will be valid for 10 years from the date of issue. For a person under 16 years of age the passport processing fee is $40, the application execution fee is $30 and the security surcharge is $12. The passport will be valid for 5 years from the date of issue. In all cases, an additional $60 fee is charged when expedited service is requested by the applicant.

CLERICAL ASSISTANT

For applicants with US Government or military authorization for no-fee passports, no fees are charged except the execution fee when applying at a designated acceptance facility.

If the applicant provides an e-mail address, passport services will only use that information to contact the applicant in the event there is a problem with the application or if the applicant needs to provide additional information to the passport agency. Applicants born in the United States must submit a previous US passport or certified birth certificate. A birth certificate must include your given name and surname, date, and place of birth, date the birth record was filed, and the seal or other certification of the official custodian of such records. Applicants born outside the United States must submit a previous US passport or Certificate of Naturalization, or Certificate of Citizenship, or Report of Birth Abroad.

SITUATION:

Your duties as a Court Assistant include filling-in for the Court Assistant assigned to the US Passport counter at the County Clerk's Office. While you are staffing that counter, George Monroe (15 years old) and his 42 years' old father, Robert Monroe, both born in the U.S., ask you some questions relating to the issuance of passports. Based on the above procedure, what is the correct response for each of the following questions?

91. Mr. Robert Monroe asks, "To obtain passports for both myself and my son, what is the total amount of fees that I need to pay?"

   A. $189.00

   B. $194.00

   C. $179.00

   D. $164.00

92. Mr. Robert Monroe asks, "One of my other sons, Jason, will apply for a passport next month and will need the passport on an expedited basis. He is 16 years old. How much will he have to pay?"

   A. $82.00

   B. $92.00

   C. $142.00

   D. None of the above.

CLERICAL ASSISTANT

93. When Mr. Monroe comes to apply for his 16 years' old son's passport, he must bring with him:

   A. $30.00 if he wishes the passport to be expedited.

   B. a copy of his son's birth certificate.

   C. an e-mail address for himself or his son.

   D. his son's previous passport or his son's certified birth certificate.

94. Mr. Monroe asks "I have a third son, William, who is 13 and wishes to apply for a passport. Do my wife and I and my son have to appear in person when applying?"

   A. No, only if he was under the age of 10.

   B. No, in all cases.

   C. Yes, because he is under 14.

   D. Yes, only If he resides with his father and mother.

95. **PROCEDURE:**

An ACD (Adjournment in Contemplation of Dismissal) may be ordered by a Judge in a Criminal Court and Family Court proceeding. An ACD adjourns the case for a six-month period. At the end of that period the case is automatically dismissed unless the DA in a criminal court case, or the Corporation Counsel in a Family Court case, have requested that the case be restored to the calendar. A case is usually restored to the calendar when the defendant in a criminal case or the respondent in a Family Court case have committed an additional offense during the six-month period. If the case is not restored to the calendar during the six-month period, the case is automatically dismissed and the court papers are sealed. If the papers are sealed, they may only be unsealed by a court order. Sealed papers may only be viewed without a court order by the original defendant in the criminal case or the respondent in the Family Court case. The issuance of an ACD by the court is not a finding of wrongdoing and is not a conviction.

CLERICAL ASSISTANT

SITUATION:

You are a Court Assistant assigned to the Queens Criminal Court information counter. Grace Smith, a member of the public, asks to see a criminal court case file on which an ACD had been issued.

95. Based on the above procedure and situation, which of the following statements is correct?
    A. Grace Smith may see the file in all cases.
    B. Grace Smith may not see the file unless she is related to the defendant in the case.
    C. Grace Smith may see the file if the papers have been unsealed by a court order.
    D. Grace Smith may not see the file, even if she was the defendant in the case.

Questions 96 - 100

Answer questions 96 - 100 based on the tables below which contain employee information and codes.

CLERICAL ASSISTANT

Employee Codes

Last Name, First Name	Court Where Assigned	County of Residence	Pension Tier	Union Representation	Health Insurance
Jefferson, Margaret	T	M	2	4	6
Lehrer, Charles	R	D	4	5	3
Ruiz, Maria	F	W	2	6	4
Wang, Matthew	S	W	2	2	2
Marino, Brendan	R	B	3	3	3
Molson, Grace	X	K	6	6	4
Braker, Leonora	F	B	3	3	3
Furstein, Janice	C	K	5	2	5

Employee Codes Explanation

Court Where Assigned	County of Residence	Pension Tier
C = Civil (Lower) T = County Court X = Civil (Supreme) F = Family R = Criminal (Lower) S = Surrogates	K = Kings Q = Queens W = Westchester D = Dutchess M = Richmond B = Bronx	2 = Tier 2 3 = Tier 3 4 = Tier 4 5 = Tier 5 6 = Tier 6
Union Representation 1 = FHAA 2 = DJFIA 3 = CONYP 4 = CIBSA 5 = HDUTS 6 = EADRS	**Health Insurance** 1 = NYEPA 2 = ACRBD 3 = NYAWN 4 = BTHSD 5 = ACECA	Codes are in this order: Court Where Employed, County of Residence, Pension Tier, Union, Health Insurance Example: CB353 (Civil (Lower), Bronx, Tier 3, HUDTS, NYAWN)

CLERICAL ASSISTANT

96. Which of the following unions was not selected by the employees listed in the preceding list?

A. DJFIA

B. CIBSA

C. FHAA

D. CONYP

97. What is the total number of employees that live in the Bronx or Westchester?

A. 2

B. 4 (2 + 2 = 4)

C. 5

D. 3

98. A new employee is scheduled to start work today at the Family Court. He lives in Bronx County and is in Pension Tier 6. He has chosen to be represented by the CONYP union and has signed up with ACECA Health Insurance. Based on the preceding, which of the following is his correct employee code?

A. FM535

B. FR365

C. RM635

D. FB635

99. A new employee is assigned to Criminal (Lower) Court and she lives in Westchester County. The first two letters of her employee code are_____.

A. RM

B. RC

C. RW

D. CR

100. Which of the following two employee codes are for employees that are in Pension Tier 3?

A. RQ3CONYP4 and XK5CONYP4

B. SM4FHAA2 and RQ3CONYP4

C. RQ3CONYP4 and SM4FHAA2

D. RB333 and FB333

End

CLERICAL ASSISTANT

PRACTICE TEST ANSWERS 11

Try to take this test (untimed) and at one sitting. The actual test may be 3-4 hours long. After the test, review any questions or types of questions that you found difficult. (Practice makes perfect!)

PRACTICE TEST
ANSWERS FOR PRACTICE TEST
(Answers are in bold and underlined.)

1. On Monday 360 new employees started working for the NYS Unified Court System. Of those new employees, 40 per cent of them live within New York City. The number of employees who live within New York City is:
A. 124   **B. 144**   C. 164   D. None of the above

2. In family court, Part A, there were 60 cases scheduled. In Part B there were 87 cases scheduled. In the entire family court there are a total of 289 cases scheduled. How many cases are scheduled in parts other than A and B?
A. 124   B. 144   C. 147   **D. None of the above** (142)

3. In the file room there are 900 files. Your supervisor tells you to take out 20 per cent of the files and put them in the next room. How many files should you put into the next room?
A. 18   B. 108   **C. 180**   D. None of the above

4. In the file room there are 3,640 files. Your job is to divide the files into four equal stacks so that each stack can be put into a separate room. How many files must each stack contain?
A. 91   B. 901   **C. 910**   D. None of the above

5. Select the best answer: The choice which contains the closest two equal amounts is:
A. .30 and 1/3   **B. 33.333% and 1/3**   C. .10 and 1/11   D. 22 per cent and 1/5

CLERICAL ASSISTANT

6. A supervisor distributes for processing 30 cases to each of his six employees. If the supervisor originally had 200 cases, how many cases remain undistributed?
A. 24
B. 20
C. 180
D. None of the above

7. On Monday 84 phone inquiries were handled by the Special Term Office. On Tuesday 93 telephone inquiries were handled by the Special Term Office. If the total number of phone inquiries handled by the Special Term Office for Monday, Tuesday and Wednesday were 283, how many telephone inquiries were handled on Wednesday?
A. 96
B. 106
C. 116
D. None of the above

8. A total of 450 cases were processed on Monday. Of those cases, 150 were processed by James Wilkins. The remainder of the cases were processed equally by Lorraine Hawkins and Jane Chin. How many cases did Lorraine Hawkins and Jane Chin each process?
A. 100
B. 125
C. 300
D. 150

9. The Judgments supervisor hands each of his nine employee 32 judgments to process. The total number of judgments which the supervisor handed out is:
A. 32
B. 9
C. 287
D. 288

10. An examination had 50 questions, with each correct answer worth 2 per cent of the final score. Kevin answered 42 questions correctly. His final score on the test is:
A. 42
B. 48
C. 80
D. 84

11. A court receives 270 cases for processing. If one employee can process 45 cases a day, how many days will that employee need to process all the 270 cases?
A. 5
B. 6
C. 7
D. None of the above

12. Adam processed 40 cases. Bob processed 50 cases. Cynthia processed 55 cases. David processed 55 cases. The average number of cases processed by Adam, Bob, Cynthia and David is:
A. 45
B. 50
C. 55
D. 54

13. The Supreme Court in Kings County received 1040 cases in one week. Because of the large number of cases received, twenty per cent were sent to the NYC Civil Court for processing. How many case did the Supreme Court in Kings County send to the NYC Civil Court?
A. 208
B. 20
C. 200
D. None of the above

CLERICAL ASSISTANT

14. Which of the following is 1/4 of 10,860?

A. 2715   B. 2751   C. 2710   D. None of the above

15. Choose the best answer: Ten court officers are assigned to security posts. Twenty court officers are assigned to courtrooms. If the total court officers assigned, what per cent is assigned to security posts?

A. 33.333 per cent   B. 25 per cent   C. 30%   D. None of the above

---

For questions 16 - 20 below, compare the three sets of information and mark your answer sheet with the correct choice, as follows:

A. Only the second and third sets are exactly alike.
B. Only the first and third sets are exactly alike.
C. None of the sets are exactly alike.
D. All three sets are exactly alike.

ANSWER

16. C.R. Ed Hymowitz SS# 892-45-8193 Family Court (1837) 372-38 129th Street FCA 3 (192.37)	C.R. Ed Hymowitz SS# 892-45-8193 Family Court (1837) 372-38 129th Street FCA 3 (192.73)	C.R. Ed Hymowitz SS# 892-45-8193 Family Court (1837) 372-38 129th Street FCA 3 (192.37)	**B**
17. J. James Holbrook C.O. Brannigan, H. 765429759-38729A Part 5, Part 8 KCV 62849/01	J. James Holbrook C.O. Brannigan, H. 765429759-38729 Part 5, Part 8 KCV 62849/01	J. James Holbrook C.O. Brannigan, H. 765429759-38729A Part 2, Part 8 KCV 62849/01	**C**
18. HC2948.KA83214 Kerns, Leonard CPLR and FCA C98621/8398/25 Doubleday, NY (99)	HC2948.KA83214 Kerns, Leonard CPLR and FCA C98621/8398/25 Doubleday, NY (99)	HC2948.KA83214 Kerns, Leonard CPLR and FCA C98621/8398/25 Doubleday, NY (99)	**D**
19. Civ Procedure Law CPL 325.46, a & d Dickerson, Evelyn 9/26/99, 2/16/01 SCK 10385/01	Civ Procedure Law CPL 325.46, a & b Dickerson, Evelyn 9/26/99, 2/16/01 SCK 10385/01	Civ Procedure Law CPL 325.46, a & b Dickerson, Evelyn 9/26/99, 2/16/01 SCK 10385/01	**A**

CLERICAL ASSISTANT

20. <u>Jenkins</u>, Richard   <u>Jenkinz</u>, Richard   <u>Jenkins</u>, Richard
    NY Laws and Rules   NY Laws and Rules   NY Laws and Rules
    NY7349.72 (c)   NY7349.72 (c)   NY7349.72 (c)   **B**
    USA Med. Mal.   USA Med. Mal.   USA Med. Mal.
    USACL01/6927342   USACL01/6927342   USACL01/6927342

For questions 21 - 30, compare the three sets of information and mark your answer sheet with the correct choice, as follows:

A. Only the first and second sets are exactly alike.
B. None of the sets are exactly alike.
C. Only the second and third sets are exactly alike.
D. All three sets are exactly alike.

21. Kiefer, Mohammud   HGSN90274365   Urly & Devry, P.C.
    HGSN90274365   Kiefer, Mohammud   Sept. 27, 1998
    Urly & Devry, P.C.   Sept. 27, 1998   Civ01/<u>321761</u>   **A**
    Sept. 27, 1998   Civ01/<u>32761</u>   Kiefer, Mohammud
    Civ01/<u>32761</u>   Urly & Devry, P.C.   HGSN90274365

22. OCR Peter Wong   Pt. 21 (9:25 AM)   J. Larry Oberman
    Pt. 21 (9:25 AM)   OCR Peter Wong   SCK7823/98 (38)
    J. Larry Oberman   SCK7823/98 (38)   OCR Peter Wong   **D**
    SCK7823/98 (38)   J. Larry Oberman   Pt. 21 (9:25 AM)

23. SC (NY) 111 Centre   Sgt. K. <u>Elvison</u>   S#: <u>869436829-38</u>
    7 Magnetometers   S#: <u>869438629-38</u>   SC (NY) 111 Centre
    Sgt. K. <u>Elvison</u>   SC (NY) 111 Centre   7 Magnetometers   **B**
    S#: <u>869436829-38</u>   7 Magnetometers   Sgt. K. <u>Elvisson</u>

24. Hayt and Wryer, PC   Hayt and Wryer, PC   Hayt and Wryer, PC
    26 Court St. 17D   Wed. 7/28/01 9AM   Wed. 7/28/01 9AM
    Wed. 7/28/01 9AM   26 Court St. 17D   Pt. 18C (<u>J. Parson</u>)   **C**
    Pt. 18C (<u>J. Parsons</u>)   Pt. 18C (<u>J. Parson</u>)   26 Court St. 17D

25. CPL389.2671(B)   37538765-498   FCA, CPLR (a)
    37538765-498   Peters, Hannah   CPL389.2671(B)
    Peters, Hannah   CPL389.2671(B)   Peters, Hannah   **D**
    FCA, CPLR (a)   FCA, CPLR (a)   37538765-498

CLERICAL ASSISTANT

26. JLK:03542987392   Law Publ., Inc.   1/13/02 (Pt. 5)
    Law Publ., Inc.   JLK:03542987392   LV65921.45629
    1/13/02 (Pt. 2)   LV65921.45629   JLK:03542987392   **C**
    LV65921.45629   1/13/02 (Pt. 5)   Law Publ., Inc.

27. ID 25649/01   293 E. 28th Ave.   L2897369.7231
    J. Ed Tremont   L2897369.7231   J. Ed Tremont
    293 E. 28th Ave.   ID 52649/01   293 E. 28th St.   **B**
    L2897369.7231   J. Ed Tremont   ID 25649/01

28. CO Lorna J. Kim   CO Lorna J. Kim   DCAS PON7189
    CR Mark S. Lipsky   S2839.82010251   CR Mark S. Lipsky
    S2839.82010251   DCAS PON7189   CO Lorna J. Kim   **A**
    DCAS PON7189   CR Mark S. Lipsky   S283982010251

29. Fleming V ZBR   J. Salamin, R.   PC73529.2819
    CFK125712/01   PC73529.2819   Fleming V ZBR
    J. Salamin, R.   CFK125721/01   J. Salamin, R.   **C**
    PC73529.2819   Fleming V ZBR   CFK125721/01

30. SS876092.782   7/24/99 & 12/3/01   SS876092.782
    DN7389/199   SS876092.782   DN7389/199
    7/24/99 & 12/3/01   DN7389/199   7/24/99 & 12/3/01   **D**
    Durston, Nicholas   Durston, Nicholas   Durston, Nicholas

For questions 31 - 35, compare the three sets of information and mark your answer sheet with the correct choice, as follows:

A. Only the first and second sets are exactly alike.
B. None of the sets are exactly alike.
C. Only the second and third sets are exactly alike.
D. All three sets are exactly alike.

31. *FCA and CPL Law*   ASF638.B293   *FCA and CPL Law*
    JBN538549276   **Ruljower, Erik**   **JBN538549276**   **D**
    ASF638.B293   *JBN538549276*   *Ruljower, Erik*
    Ruljower, Erik   FCA and CPL Law   **ASF638.B293**

32. ALBERMARLE RD. 16   PET. KYLE ROUTER   *127 Liv. St. 7F-252*
    PET. KYLE ROUTER   *127 Liv. St. 7F-252*   Albermarl Rd. 16
    127 LIV. ST. 7F-252   Albermarle Rd. 16   Pet. Kyle Router   **A**

CLERICAL ASSISTANT

SEC8273955.4629	SEC8273955.4629	SEC8273955.4629	
33. 425-52 W. 129 Ave. *Priority* <u>7F97312</u> *Aided K01/078-9* *OSHA 37485726*	**AIDED K01/078-9** **OSHA 37485726** **425-52 W. 129 AVE.** **PRIORITY** <u>7F93712</u>	Priority <u>7F93712</u> *Aided K01/078-9* 425-52 W. 129 Ave. **OSHA 37485726**	**C**
34. Fredericks, Bill **Apex BP, Inc.** Criminal Law <u>X93717197321</u>	Apex BP, Inc. Criminal Law **Fredericks, Bill** <u>X93717197321</u>	<u>X937171197321</u> *Fredericks, Bill* Apex BP, Inc. **Criminal Law**	**A**
31. *SFCA and CPL Law* JBN538539276 **ASF638.B293** **Ruljower, Erik**	ASF638.B293 **Ruljower, Erik** *JBN538539276* SFCA and CPL Law	SFCA and CPL Law **JBN538539276** *Ruljower, Erik* **ASF638.B293**	**D**

CLERICAL ASSISTANT

Questions 36 - 45:
Below is a list of employees, the date each was hired, employee ID number and department.
First, prepare 4 lists of the employees in
   1. alphabetical order by last name
   2. Employee Number (numerical order)
   3. date hired order
   4. department order (alphabetical order of departments with alphabetical list of employees within that department).
After preparing the above lists, answer the 10 questions that follow. (You will not be graded on the lists. You will only be graded on your answers to the 10 questions).

NAME	DATE HIRED	EMPLOYEE NUMBER	DEPARTMENT
Worth, Jules	5/17/2003	66892	Judgments
Jordan, James	6/3/1987	88234	Warrants
Grodin, Bill	3/4/1978	34889	Small Claims
Patterson, Leonard	8/8/1998	00273	Judgments
Aikens, Kim	5/5/1983	45999	Special Term
Yard, William	2/9/2002	54908	Landlord and Tenant
Osgood, Jill	5/6/1988	37890	Special Term
Dartmouth, Kim	6/1/1984	18767	Calendar
Heniken, Eleanor	5/6/2002	99012	Warrants
Quigly, Norma	6/5/1976	82098	Special Term
Roller, Francine	3/7/2004	34567	Judgments
Zales, David	2/2/2003	51435	Calendar
Vanguard, George	5/4/1974	88657	Calendar
Dundee, Robert	7/5/1997	35912	Landlord and Tenant
Minkin, Lena	8/4/1982	87777	General Clerk
Feinstein, Pat	4/3/2003	29329	Special Term
Brinks, Sam	3/5/2001	81432	Landlord and Tenant
Joones, Erik	4/2/1988	77953	Judgments
United, Frank	2/7/2002	32598	Judgments
Paline, Thomas	5/2/1996	63999	Warrants
Wonkin, Paul	9/9/1987	44876	General Clerk
Chin, Robert	2/2/1995	34354	Small Claims
Kevany, Pamela	6/4/1977	96345	Judgments
Ericson, Vivian	8/4/1999	89876	Special Term
Battle, James	4/1/1986	10241	Appeals

CLERICAL ASSISTANT

Examples of the completed worksheets are as follows

Alphabetical order by last name

a Aikens	b Battle Brinks	c Chin	d Dartmouth Dundee
e Ericson	f Feinstein	g Grodin	h Heniken
i	j Joones Jordan	k Kevany	l
m Minkin	n	o Osgood	p Paline Patterson
q Quigly	r Roller	s	t
u United	v Vanguard	w Wonkin Worth	x

y   Yard   z   Zales

1. Aikens
2. Battle
3. Brinks
4. Chin
5. Dartmouth
6. Dundee
7. Ericson
8. Feinstein
9. Grodin
10. Heniken
11. Joones
12. Jordan
13. Kevany
14. Minikin
15. Osgood
16. Paline
17. Patterson
18. Quigly
19. Roller
20. United
21. Vanguard
22. Wonkin
23. Worth
24. Yard
25. Zales

CLERICAL ASSISTANT

Employee Number (numerical order)

0-10,000	10,001-20,000	20,001-30,000	30,001-40,000	40,001-50,000
00273	10241	29329	32958	44876
	18767		34354	45999
			34567	
			34889	
			35912	
			37890	

50,001-60,000	60,001-70,000	70,001-80,000	80,001-90,000	90,001-100,000
51435	63999	77953	81432	96345
54908	66892		82098	99012
			87777	
			88234	
			88657	
			89876	

1. 00273
2. 10241
3. 18767
4. 29329
5. 32958
6. 34354
7. 34567
8. 34889
9. 35912
10. 37890
11. 44876
12. 45999
13. 51435
14. 54908
15. 63999
16. 66892
17. 77953
18. 81432
19. 82098
20. 87777
21. 88234
22. 88657
23. 89876
24. 96345
25. 99012

CLERICAL ASSISTANT

Date Hired Order

1970s	1980s	1990s	2000s
5-4-74	8-4-82	2-2-95	3-5-2001
6-5-76	5-5-83	5-2-96	2-7-2002
6-4-77	6-1-84	7-5-97	2-9-2002
3-4-78	4-1-86	8-8-98	5-6-2002
	6-3-87	8-4-99	2-2-2003
	9-9-87		4-3-2003
	4-2-88		5-17-2003
	5-6-88		3-7-2004

1. 5-4-74
2. 6-5-76
3. 6-4-77
4. 3-4-78
5. 8-4-82
6. 5-5-83
7. 6-1-84
8. 4-1-86
9. 6-3-87
10. 9-9-87
11. 4-2-88
12. 5-6-88
13. 2-2-95
14. 5-2-96
15. 7-5-97
16. 8-8-98
17. 8-4-99
18. 3-5-2001
19. 2-07-2002
20. 2-9-2002
21. 5-6-2002
22. 2-2-2003
23. 4-3-2003
24. 5-17-2003
25. 3-7-2004

CLERICAL ASSISTANT

Department order (and alphabetical order of employees in alphabetized departments)

Appeals	
Battle	
Calendar	
Dartmouth	
Vanguard	
Zales	
General Clerk	
Minikin	
Wonkin	
Judgments	
Joones	
Kevany	
Patterson	
Roller	
United	
Worth	
Landlord a& Tenant	
Brinks	
Dundee	
Yard	
Small Claims	
Chin	
Grodin	
Special Term	
Aikens	
Ericson	
Feinstein	
Osgood	
Quigly	
Warrants	
Heniken	
Jordan	
Paline	

1. Appeals Battle
2. Calendar Dartmouth
3. Vanguard
4. Zales
5. General Clerk Miniken
6. Wonkin
7. Judgments Joones
8. Kevany
9. Patterson
10. Roller
11. United
12. Worth
13. Landlord and Tenant Brinks
14. Dundee
15. Yard
16. Small Claims Chin
17. Grodin
18. Special Term Aikens
19. Ericson
20. Feinstein
21. Osgood
22. Quigly
23. Warrants Henikin
24. Jordan
25. Paline

CLERICAL ASSISTANT

36. The tenth name in the Last Name Alphabetical File is:
A. Fernstein   B. Grodin   **C. Heniken**   D. Joones

37. The twenty-second name in the Last Name Alphabetical File is:
A. Wonkir   B. Vanguard   C. Worth   **D. Wonkin**

38. Which of the following four statements is not correct?
A. Zales is the last name in the Last Name Alphabetical File.
B. Feinstein is the eighth name in the Last Name Alphabetical File.
C. Dundee is the sixth name in the Last Name Alphabetical file.
D. Jordan is the fourteenth name in the Last Name Alphabetical File.

39. The employee whose hired date is listed number 6 on the chronological date hired list is:
A. Minkin, Lena   **B. Aikens, Kim**   C. Dartmouth, Jim   D. None of the above

40. The name of the employee whose employee number is listed number 18 on the chronological employee number list is ____:
A. Kevany, Pamela
B. Brinks, Sam
C. Jameson, Erik
D. Vanguard, George

41. Employee Robert Chin's employee number is listed number ___ on the list of employee numbers.
A. 6   B. 7   C. 8   D. 9

42. The employee whose employee number is number 10 on the chronological list of employee numbers works in the ___ department.
A. General Clerk   **B. Special Term**   C. Calendar   D. Small Claims

43. Employee number 82098 is listed number ___ on the chronological list of employee numbers.
A. 19   B. 20   C. 18   D. 21

44. The name of the employee that is listed last on the chronological list of employee numbers is named:
A. Battle, James   **B. Heniken, Eleanor**   C. Worth, Jules   D. Zales, David

45. The number of employees assigned to the Judgments department is:
A. 4   B. 5   C. 7   **D. None of the above (6)**

For questions 46 - 60, read the paragraph and then choose the word which best fits in each of the underlined spaces.

CLERICAL ASSISTANT

A person of average __46__ cannot move the chair. The reason for this is that the chair weighs over 200 pounds. Also, a person of average __47__ cannot see over the wall. The chair and the wall, therefore, are in __48__ of ADA requirements and therefore must be corrected to avoid a fine. The federal inspector will __49__ in 60 days to inspect the site once again.

46. A. height   B. temperament   C. weight   **D. strength**
47. A. strength   B. weight   C. temperament   **D. height**
48. A. concurrence   B. agreement   C. tandem   **D. violation**
49. A. sojourn   B. respect   **C. return**   D. detour

The account of the witness was __50__ to believe. The reason for this is that there was no light in the room and therefore no way for him to see who broke the vase. The fingerprint analysis is a much __51__ indicator of who is guilty. Fingerprints are unique and when __52__ to those on the broken pieces, provide reasonable cause to believe who broke the vase.

50. A. easy   B. likely   **C. hard**   D. not
51. A. less   B. more   C. worse   **D. better**
52. A. differed   B. differentiated   **C. matched**   D. dissolved

The new Court Officer and the young litigant __53__ going to be here tomorrow morning. Please have the subpoenaed records ready for them. The attorneys __54__ also authorized to see them. Copies may be made by them. However, the original documents may not be __55__ out of the record room.

53. A. is   B. was   **C. are**   D. isn't
54. A. is   **B. are**   C. was   D. aren't
55. A. brought   B. taking   **C. taken**   D. takened

Perhaps one indicator of truly enlightened court administration is __56__ on quality public service. Lacking the historic "profit motive" for emphasizing quality public service, the enlightened court administrator does so __57__ for the public good than any financial gain.

56. A. avoidance   B. seeking   C. diminishing   **D. emphasis**
57. A. less   B. because   **C. more**   D. seeking

Alternative dispute resolution (ADR) is a __58__ by which parties in a dispute seek resolution of their dispute without a court trial. Two methods used in ADR are mediation and arbitration. Unless otherwise agreed to, parties __59__ participate in mediation and arbitration do not give up __60__ right to submit their controversy to a court for trial.

58. A. procedures   **B. process**   C. attempts   D. prescriptions
59. A. which   B. whom   **C. who**   D. too
60. A. his   **B. their**   C. her   D. your

CLERICAL ASSISTANT

The following table applies to questions 71-75. Before answering the questions, complete the partially filled-in table based on the partial information provided.

SUMMARY OF CASES Terms 1 - 5						
Case Activity	Term 1	Term 2	Term 3	Term 4	Term 5	Total Number of Cases
Adjourned	6	**4**	2	5	3	20
Defaulted	2	4	3	1	**5**	15
Dismissed	3	1	3	2	3	**12**
Settled - with money award	4	6	4	**7**	5	**26**
Settled - with no money award	**3**	1	3	2	2	11
Total Number of Cases On Calendar	18	16	**15**	17	**18**	84

61. What is the total number of cases adjourned during Term 3?
    A. 20 B. 16 C. 17 D. 18

62. What is the total number of dismissed cases?
    A. 10 B. 11 **C. 12** D. 13

63. What is the total number of cases "settled - with money award" and "settled - with no money award"?
    A. 35 B. 36 **C. 37** D. 38

64. What is the total number of "defaulted" and "dismissed" cases?
    A. 26 **B. 27** C. 28 D. 29

65. Which term had the least number of cases on the calendar?
    A. Term 2 **B. Term 3** C. Term 4 D. Term 5

CLERICAL ASSISTANT

Using the information in table 1, complete tables 2, 3 and 4, and then answer questions 66-85 based on the information in tables 1 - 4.

	DAILY CASE LOG					Table 1
	Monday - Friday					
Part	Case Type	Date Filed	Day Appeared On Court Calendar	Case Status	Money Award	Fine
Part 1	Civil	3/16/98	Monday	Dismissed	X	
Part 2	Civil	7/9/97	Monday	Settled	X	
Part 1	Criminal	5/16/98	Monday	Trial completed		$5,000
Part 3	Civil	3/21/99	Monday	Settled	X	
Part 4	Criminal	9/24/00	Monday	Trial completed		X
Part 5	Civil	4/13/97	Tuesday	Dismissed	X	
Part 6	Criminal	12/24/00	Tuesday	Trial completed		$3,000
Part 7	Civil	2/7/96	Tuesday	Settled	$7,500	
Part 1	Criminal	5/21/01	Tuesday	Trial completed		X
Part 3	Criminal	5/21/01	Tuesday	Adjourned		X
Part 6	Civil	7/26/98	Tuesday	Settled	$21,500	
Part 5	Civil	2/15/97	Wednesday	Settled	X	
Part 4	Civil	12/9/98	Wednesday	Settled	$5,400	
Part 5	Civil	3/16/97	Wednesday	Defaulted	X	
Part 5	Civil	4/22/98	Wednesday	Adjourned	X	
Part 1	Criminal	4/12/99	Thursday	Trial completed		$3,000
Part 6	Civil	4/14/99	Thursday	Adjourned	X	
Part 3	Civil	6/24/98	Thursday	Settled	$2,400	
Part 4	Civil	3/7/97	Thursday	Dismissed	X	
Part 5	Civil	1/26/98	Friday	Defaulted	X	
Part 3	Criminal	4/21/98	Friday	Adjourned		X
Part 1	Civil	5/26/96	Friday	Settled	$1,500	

CLERICAL ASSISTANT

SUMMARY OF CASES — Table 2

Monday - Friday

Case Activity	Monday	Tuesday	Wednesday	Thursday	Friday	Total Number of Cases
Adjourned		1	1	1	1	4
Defaulted			1		1	2
Dismissed	1	1		1		3
Settled - with money award		2	1	1	1	5
Settled - with no money award	2		1			3
Trial completed - with fine	1	1		1		3
Trial completed - with no fine	1	1				2
Total Number of Cases On Calendar	5	6	4	4	3	22

Table 3 — **SUMMARY OF CASES (BY YEAR FILED)**

Monday - Friday

Year Filed	Monday	Tuesday	Wed.	Thursday	Friday	Total Number of Cases
1996		1			1	2
1997	1	1	2	1		5
1998	2	1	2	1	2	8
1999	1			2		3
2000	1	1				2
2001		2				2
Total Number of Cases	5	6	4	4	3	22

CLERICAL ASSISTANT

SUMMARY OF CASES (BY PART) — Table 4
Monday - Friday

Part	Adjourned	Dismissed	De-faulted	Settled - with no money award	Settled - with money award	Trial completed- no fine	Trial completed - with fine	Total Cases
1		1			1	1	2	5
2				1				1
3	2			1	1			4
4		1			1	1		3
5	1	1	2	1				5
6	1					1	1	3
7						1		1
Total	4	3	2	3	5	2	3	22

66. How many cases were filed during 1997?
A. 4 **B. 5** C. 6 D. 7

67. How many cases were settled on Tuesday and Wednesday with a money award?
A. 1 B. 2 **C. 3** D. 4

68. What is the total number of cases adjourned or defaulted on Wednesday?
A. 1 **B. 2** C. 3 D. 4

69. How many cases were settled on Monday and Tuesday with no money award?
A. 3 **B. 2** C. 1 D. 0

70. What is the total number of cases adjourned by Part 1 and Part 5?
A. 1 B. 2 C. 3 D. 4

71. Which Part has the greatest number of adjourned cases?
A. Part 6 B. Part 4 **C. Part 3** D. Part 5

72. Which Parts have more cases "Settled - with money award" than they have cases "Settled - with no money award?"
A. Parts 1, 4, 6 and 7 B. Parts 1, 6 and 7 C. Parts 4, 6 and 7 D. Part 1, 4 and 7

73. What is the total number of cases "Settled-with no money award" and "Settled-with money award"?
A. 8 B. 9 C. 10 D. 11

CLERICAL ASSISTANT

74. The total number of cases filed in 1996 and 1998 is?
A. 12
B. 13
C. 11
D. 10

75. Which Part has the greatest number of defaulted cases?
A. Part 5
B. Part 4
C. Part 3
D. Part 2

76. The total of cases "Settled - with money award" exceeded the total of cases "Settled - with no money award" by:
A. 3
B. 4
C. 2
D. 6

77. Total number of cases Dismissed and Defaulted exceeded the total number of cases adjourned by:
A. 1
B. 2
C. 3
D. 4

78. Choose the best answer: Cases filed in 1996 appeared on the calendar on which days?
A. Monday
B. Tuesday
C. Thursday and Friday
D. Tuesday and Friday

79. What is the total number of cases filed in 1998 and 1997?
A. 9
B. 10
C. 12
D. 13

80. The three Parts which had more than three cases on the calendar were:
A. Parts 1, 5 and 7
B. Parts 1, 3 and 5
C. Parts 3, 5 and 6
D. Parts 2, 5 and 7

81. The Part which had the greatest number of case "Trial completed - with fine" was:
A. Part 1
B. Part 2
C. Part 3
D. Part 4

82. The number of "Trials completed - with fine" exceeds the number of "Trials completed - no fine" by:
A. 4
B. 3
C. 2
D. 1

83. The total number of cases Monday - Friday was:
A. 6
B. 22
C. 8
D. 9

84. The year in which exactly 3 cases were filed is:
A. 1998
B. 1999
C. 2000
D. 1996

85. The total number of settled cases is:
A. 6
B. 7
C. 8
D. 9

For questions 86 - 90, select the choice that is most correct in accordance with standard English grammar, usage, punctuation and sentence structure.

CLERICAL ASSISTANT

86. A. The applicant scored high because he studied dilligently.
    B. The applicant scored high because he studied diligently. (correct spelling)
    C. The applicant scored high because he studied dilegently.
    D. The applicant scored high because he studied diliggently.

87. A. The argument was between John, Eleanor and William. ("between" should be "among".)
    B. The argument was among John, Eleanor and William. (correct usage of "among".)
    C. The arguments was between John, Eleanor and William. ("arguments" is plural. "was" is singular.)
    D. The arguments is between John, Eleanor and William. ("arguments" is plural. "is" is singular.)

88. A. Its the best way to study. (Should be "it's" - meaning "It is".)
    B. Its the best ways to study. ("Its" is not correct. "Ways" should be "way".)
    C. It's the best way to study.
    D. Its' the best way to study. ("Its" should be "It's".)

89. A. The exam was difficult the proctor was young. (run-on sentence)
    B. The exam was difficult --the proctor was young. (inappropriate use of "--")
    C. The exam was difficult and the proctor was young.
    D. The exam was difficult / the proctor was young. (inappropriate use of "/".)

90. A. The bag contained the following pencils, pens, erasers and a ruler. (missing ":" after the word "following".)
    B. The bag contained the following; pencils, pens, erasers and a ruler. (";" should be ":")
    C. The bag contained the following items pencils, pens, erasers and a ruler. (missing ":" after the word "items".)
    D. The bag contained the following: pencils, pens, erasers and a ruler.

Questions 91-95

PROCEDURE: (Processing of passport application)

As directed by public law 106-119 and 22 CFR 51.27 effective July 2, 2001: To submit an application for a child under age 14, both parents or the child's legal guardian(s) must appear and present evidence of the child's US citizenship and evidence of the child's relationship to parents/guardians, and parental identification. As directed by regulation 22 CFR 51 effective February 1, 2004, each minor child applying for a passport must appear in person.

For a person who is 16 years of age or older, the passport processing fee is $55, the application execution fee is $30, and the security surcharge is $12. The passport will be valid for 10 years from the date of issue. For a person under 16 years of age the passport

CLERICAL ASSISTANT

processing fee is $40, the application execution fee is $30 and the security surcharge is $12. The passport will be valid for 5 years from the date of issue. In all cases, an additional $60 fee is charged when expedited service is requested by the applicant.

For applicants with US Government or military authorization for no-fee passports, no fees are charged except the execution fee when applying at a designated acceptance facility.

If the applicant provides an e-mail address, passport services will only use that information to contact the applicant in the event there is a problem with the application or if the applicant needs to provide additional information to the passport agency. Applicants born in the United States must submit a previous US passport or certified birth certificate. A birth certificate must include your given name and surname, date, and place of birth, date the birth record was filed, and the seal or other certification of the official custodian of such records. Applicants born outside the United States must submit a previous US passport or Certificate of Naturalization, or Certificate of Citizenship, or Report of Birth Abroad.

SITUATION:

Your duties as a Court Assistant include filling-in for the Court Assistant assigned to the US Passport counter at the County Clerk's Office. While you are staffing that counter, George Monroe (15 years old) and his 42 years' old father, Robert Monroe, both born in the U.S., ask you some questions relating to the issuance of passports. Based on the above procedure, what is the correct response for each of the following questions?

91. Mr. Robert Monroe asks, "To obtain passports for both myself and my son, what is the total amount of fees that I need to pay?"

    A. $189.00

    B. $194.00

    C. $179.00

    D. $164.00

91. C $179.00 ($55+$30+$12=97, for father...and $40+$30+$12=82, for son. Total $97 + $82 = $179).

CLERICAL ASSISTANT

92. Mr. Robert Monroe asks, "One of my other sons, Jason, will apply for a passport next month and will need the passport on an expedited basis. He is 16 years old. How much will he have to pay?"

    A. $82.00

    B. $92.00

    C. $142.00

    D. None of the above.

92. D None of the above. ($55 + $30 + $12 + expedite fee of $60 = $157.00).

93. When Mr. Monroe comes to apply for his 16 years' old son's passport, he must bring with him:

    A. $30.00 if he wishes the passport to be expedited.

    B. a copy of his son's birth certificate.

    C. an e-mail address for himself or his son.

    D. his son's previous passport or his son's certified birth certificate.

93. D his son's previous passport or his son's certified birth certificate.

94. Mr. Monroe asks "I have a third son, William, who is 13 and wishes to apply for a passport. Do my wife and I and my son have to appear in person when applying?"

    A. No, only if he was under the age of 10.

    B. No, in all cases.

    C. Yes, because he is under 14.

    D. Yes, only If he resides with his father and mother.

94. C. Yes, because he is a minor under 14.

95. **PROCEDURE:**

An ACD (Adjournment in Contemplation of Dismissal) may be ordered by a Judge in a Criminal Court and Family Court proceeding. An ACD adjourns the case for a six-month period. At the end of that period the case is automatically dismissed unless the DA in a

CLERICAL ASSISTANT

criminal court case, or the Corporation Counsel in a Family Court case, have requested that the case be restored to the calendar. A case is usually restored to the calendar when the defendant in a criminal case or the respondent in a Family Court case have committed an additional offense during the six-month period. If the case is not restored to the calendar during the six-month period, the case is automatically dismissed and the court papers are sealed. If the papers are sealed, they may only be unsealed by a court order. Sealed papers may only be viewed without a court order by the original defendant in the criminal case or the respondent in the Family Court case. The issuance of an ACD by the court is not a finding of wrongdoing and is not a conviction.

SITUATION:

You are a Court Assistant assigned to the Queens Criminal Court information counter. Grace Smith, a member of the public, asks to see a criminal court case file on which an ACD had been issued.

95. Based on the above procedure and situation, which of the following statements is correct?
   A. Grace Smith may see the file in all cases.
   B. Grace Smith may not see the file unless she is related to the defendant in the case.
   C. Grace Smith may see the file if the papers have been unsealed by a court order.
   D. Grace Smith may not see the file, even if she was the defendant in the case.

95. C. Grace Smith may see the file if the papers have been unsealed by a court order.

Questions 96 - 100

Answer questions 96-100 based on the tables below which contain employee information and codes.

CLERICAL ASSISTANT

Employee Codes

Last Name, First Name	Court Where Assigned	County of Residence	Pension Tier	Union Representation	Health Insurance
Jefferson, Margaret	T	M	2	4	6
Lehrer, Charles	R	D	4	5	3
Ruiz, Maria	F	W	2	6	4
Wang, Matthew	S	W	2	2	2
Marino, Brendan	R	B	3	3	3
Molson, Grace	X	K	6	6	4
Braker, Leonora	F	B	3	3	3
Furstein, Janice	C	K	5	2	5

Employee Codes Explanation

Court Where Assigned

C = Civil (Lower)
T = County Court
X = Civil (Supreme)
F = Family
R = Criminal (Lower)
S = Surrogates

County of Residence

K = Kings
Q = Queens
W = Westchester
D = Dutchess
M = Richmond
B = Bronx

Pension Tier

2 = Tier 2
3 = Tier 3
4 = Tier 4
5 = Tier 5
6 = Tier 6

Union Representation

1 = FHAA
2 = DJFIA
3 = CONYP
4 = CIBSA
5 = HDUTS
6 = EADRS

Health Insurance

1 = NYEPA
2 = ACRBD
3 = NYAWN
4 = BTHSD
5 = ACECA

Codes are in this order: Court Where Employed, County of Residence, Pension Tier, Union, Health Insurance

Example:
CB353
(Civil (Lower), Bronx, Tier 3, HUDTS, NYAWN)

CLERICAL ASSISTANT

96. Which of the following unions was not selected by the employees listed in the preceding list?

A. DJFIA

B. CIBSA

C. FHAA

D. CONYP

97. What is the total number of employees that live in the Bronx or Westchester?

A. 2

B. 4 (2 + 2 = 4)

C. 5

D. 3

98. A new employee is scheduled to start work today at the Family Court. He lives in Bronx County and is in Pension Tier 6. He has chosen to be represented by the CONYP union and has signed up with ACECA Health Insurance. Based on the preceding, which of the following is his correct employee code?

A. FM535

B. FR365

C. RM635

D. FB635

99. A new employee is assigned to Criminal (Lower) Court and she lives in Westchester County. The first two letters of her employee code are_____.

A. RM

B. RC

C. RW

D. CR

100. Which of the following two employee codes are for employees that are in Pension Tier 3?

A. RQ3CONYP4 and XK5CONYP4

B. SM4FHAA2 and RQ3CONYP4

C. RQ3CONYP4 and SM4FHAA2

D. RB333 and FB333

End

CLERICAL ASSISTANT

Practice Test Answer Key

1. B	36. C	71. C
2. D	37. D	72. A
3. C	38. D	73. A
4. C	39. B	74. D
5. B	40. B	75. A
6. B	41. A	76. C
7. B	42. B	77. A
8. D	43. A	78. D
9. D	44. B	79. D
10. D	45. D	80. B
11. B	46. D	81. A
12. B	47. D	82. D
13. A	48. D	83. B
14. A	49. C	84. B
15. A	50. C	85. C
16. B	51. D	86. B
17. C	52. C	87. B
18. D	53. C	88. C
19. A	54. B	89. C
20. B	55. C	90. D
21. A	56. D	91. C
22. D	57. C	92. D
23. B	58. B	93. D
24. C	59. C	94. C
25. D	60. B	95. C
26. C	61. A	96. C
27. B	62. C	97. B
28. A	63. C	98. D
29. C	64. B	99. C
30. D	65. B	100. D
31. D	66. B	
32. A	67. C	
33. C	68. B	
34. A	69. B	
35. D	70. A	

CLERICAL ASSISTANT

TEST-TAKING SUGGESTIONS

1. Get a good night's sleep. The night before the exam is not the time to go to a bar or to a sports game. Scientific studies have shown that sleep deprivation dulls the mind.

2. If at all possible, try not to cram. If you can, review the question exercises, practice questions, suggestions, and practice test. If you have been studying correctly, you owe it to yourself to rest. Cramming often hurts instead of helping. Pace yourself each day and you won't feel the need to sprint at the last moment.

3. Pay careful attention to the time and location of the test site, and wake up early enough so that you will have more than enough time to get there. For more than thirty years I have heard many horror stories of candidates not arriving at the test site on time.

4. At the test site, follow directions carefully and do not take anything for granted. Don't miss any information that might help you get a higher score.

5. When you are allowed to do so, check your computer for any problems.

6. Crystallize in your mind how many questions you have to answer - and also the type of questions. You might be taking a test which is given for both an entry level and promotional positions. You may be required to answer only certain specified questions in the test booklet. Make sure you know what questions you are required to answer and answer only those questions.

7. Quickly develop a time budget - and during the exam check the time on your watch to make sure you are not falling behind. Usually every question is worth the same as the other questions. Don't spend too much time on any one question (unless you have finished all the other questions and are satisfied with your answers.)

8. If you find that there are questions for which you believe there is more than one valid answer, do not lose time thinking about it. Select the best answer that you can - and go on.

9. Finally - and very important - if you finish early, do not get up and go home. Review the exam and your answers over and over again until you have no choice but to leave the room.

GOOD LUCK !!!

CLERICAL ASSISTANT

Notes

CLERICAL ASSISTANT

Notes